Tikal Report No. 37

HISTORICAL ARCHAEOLOGY AT TIKAL, GUATEMALA

MUSEUM MONOGRAPH 135

Tikal Report No. 37

HISTORICAL ARCHAEOLOGY AT TIKAL, GUATEMALA

Hattula Moholy-Nagy

Series Editors
William A. Haviland
Christopher Jones

UNIVERSITY OF PENNSYLVANIA MUSEUM OF ARCHAEOLOGY AND ANTHROPOLOGY

PHILADELPHIA

Hattula Moholy-Nagy joined the Tikal Project of the University of Pennsylvania Museum in 1960 and headed the field laboratory at Tikal from 1961 through 1964. She is currently a Consulting Scholar in the Museum's American Section.

LIBRARY OF CONGRESS CATALOGING-IN-PUBLICATION DATA

Moholy-Nagy, Hattula.
  Historical archaeology at Tikal, Guatemala / Hattula Moholy-Nagy.
    pages cm. — (Tikal report ; no. 37)
  Includes bibliographical references and index.
  ISBN 978-1-934536-47-6 (hardcover : alk. paper) — ISBN 1-934536-47-4 (hardcover : alk. paper)
  1. Tikal Site (Guatemala) 2. Excavations (Archaeology)—Guatemala—Tikal Site—History. I. Title.
  F1465.1.T5M65 2012
  972.81'2—dc23

                      2012011837

Published for the University of Pennsylvania Museum of Archaeology and Anthropology by the University of Pennsylvania Press.

Printed in the United States of America on acid-free paper.

Contents

Appendices

(A-D, L-M are located on the accompanying CD-ROM)

Figures

Color and black and white photographs not printed in the Report are located on the CD-ROM as Appendix L. Figures printed in the Report, listed below, are also located on the CD-ROM as Appendix M.

ILLUSTRATIONS IN APPENDIX L (CD)

community ceremony, the Ritual of the Skull. Food offered in religious rituals had to be cooked in pottery. Behind her is a large pottery bowl with vertical lug handles (Reina 1962:30).

L27 A kitchen in San José Petén, which is in a structure separate from the house, 1961 (Reina 1962:30). Most of the cooking and eating utensils are of metal and enameled ware, but there is also a large pottery bowl with everted rim to the left and a pottery, or perhaps gourd, bowl on the table to the right.

L28 An altar in a home in San José Petén set for the Ritual of the Skull, 1961 (Reina 1962:33). Offerings of food in enameled ware are placed on the table in front of the altar, but the meal offered to the Skull on the altar is served in traditional pottery and gourd dishes.

L29 *Jocote* trees (also known as *jobo* or *mombín*) (*Spondias,* cf. *mombin*) near the Tikal Aguada, 1998 (Palka 2005: fig. 6.20). This tree produces an edible plum-like fruit and grows naturally in the Tikal area.

L30 A *pimenta* or allspice tree (*Pimenta dioica*), indigenous to Tikal, 1998.

L31 An orange or lime tree planted by the residents of the 19th-century settlement at Tikal, 1998.

L32 A palm tree exotic to Tikal, 1998.

L33 Northern exterior of RS 5F-1, excavated as Operation 7 by the LAP, 1998 (Palka 2005: fig. 6.29). The stone perimeter of the structure, a scatter of small artifacts, some metal box strap fragments, and a large fragment of a pottery jar with loop handles in the foreground (are visible.

L34 RS 5F-1, re-excavated as Operation 7 by the LAP, 1998. The scatter of sherds and chert artifacts to the north of the structure.

L35 RS 5F-1, re-excavated as Operation 7 by the LAP, 1998. A cluster of metal box strap fragments on the floor near the stone wall footings of the structure.

L36 RS 5F-2, excavated as Operation 5 by the LAP, 1998 (Palka 2005: fig. 6.27). Hearth, on-floor scatter of sherds and chert artifacts, and large stones perhaps used as seats.

L37 RS 5F-3, excavated as Operation 3 by the LAP, 1998. Two pieces of painted white earthenware in the associated sheet midden.

L38 RS 5F-3, excavated as Operation 3 by the LAP, 1998 (Palka 2005: fig. 6.25). Scatter of sherds, metal fragments, and a gunpowder flask in the associated exterior sheet midden.

L39 Three reused Precolumbian chert artifacts from RS 5F-3, excavated as Operation 3 by the LAP. From left to right, a hammerstone, a heavily patinated biface fragment, and a large flake with a natural cavity, 1998.

L40 Expedient Precolumbian or possibly Recent chert artifacts recovered from several LAP operations, 1998.

L41 A machete fragment of the Collins type, recovered by the LAP, 1998.

L42 Barrel of a gun recovered by the LAP, 1998.

L43 Sherds of a large, plainware jar with loop handles recovered from RS 5F-1, Operation 7, by the LAP, 1998 (Palka 2005: fig. 6.29).

L44 Sherds from six plainware pottery vessels from various LAP operations, 1998.

L45 Fragment of a flaring-sided pottery bowl from RS 5F-3, LAP Operation 3, 1998.

L46 Joel W. Palka conducting the metal detector survey for the Lacandon Archaeological Project at Tikal, 1998.

L47 Dennis E. Puleston (1940–1978).

Tables

Acknowledgments

This report incorporates information, advice, and critical feedback from many helpful people over the course of more than four decades. I am especially grateful to the following:

The archaeologists and workmen who helped to excavate Recent Site 5F-1.

Marshall Becker for his translation of Salvador Valenzuela's report of 1879.

John E. Clark for the references to Prof. Walter M. Wolfe's 1901 trip to Tikal, Arlene Colman for supplying the text of Wolfe's journal, and Irene Adams, Reference Specialist, L. Tom Perry Special Collections, Harold B. Lee Library at Brigham Young University, for permission to publish it.

William R. Coe for organizing the excavation of RS 5F-1, drawing the plan and sections of Str. 5F-1, and for photographing nearly all of the recovered artifacts.

T. Patrick Culbert for analysis of pre-Columbian sherds recovered from Recent Sites.

William A. Haviland, Christopher Jones, Laura J. Kosakowsky, Joel W. Palka, and Rubén E. Reina for corrections and comments on earlier versions of this report.

Barbara Hayden for expertly inking Coe's plans and sections, proof-reading the manuscript, and essential help with the preparation of illustrations for publication.

Jennifer Quick for copy-editing and book design.

C. L. Lundell for botanical identifications of domesticated plants and information about local vegetation.

Paul S. Newton for his gracefully written reports of research on the Bottles of Tikal and permission to publish them.

Antonio and Aura Luz Ortiz, and Ciriaco Contreras for information about the uses of artifacts recovered from Recent Sites.

Joel W. Palka for information on his excavations at La Palmera, the 19th-century settlement at Tikal, permission to publish photographs of his excavations there, numerous suggestions on the manuscript, and especially for his interest and encouragement to publish these unanticipated data from Tikal.

Dennis E. Puleston for information about the coconut palm.

Rubén E. Reina for making available a study collection of pottery from San José pottery, as well as detailed ethnographic information on San José's material culture. Reina also called the Valenzuela report to our attention and corrected parts of the translation of it made by Marshall J. Becker.

Edwin M. Shook for encouragement to investigate the Recent Sites and for providing essential background information about their discovery and collection.

Two anonymous peer reviewers, especially Reviewer #1, who brought Grant Jones's book to my attention.

Elizabeth and Dante Sobrevilla for their essential help with the Spanish summary.

Roger G. Schneggenburger for his continuing patience and support.

Abbreviations

Alt.	altar
cm	centimeter
E	east
G	structure group
Gp.	structure group
km	kilometer
LAP	Lacandon Archaeological Project
m	meter
MS.	Miscellaneous Stone
N	North
NZone	North Zone
p	plaza, platform
R	Recent Site
Rd	road
RS	Recent Site
s	sub
S	South
St.	stela
Str.	Structure
TikNatPk	Tikal National Park
W	west

Introduction

In 1956 the Tikal Project of the University of Pennsylvania Museum under the direction of Edwin M. Shook (Fig. L01) established a field camp among the ancient Maya ruins in the Department of the Petén, Guatemala (Figs. 1, L02-L06; TR. 1). The Project's next task was to initiate a survey for the site map (Fig. 2; TR. 11). As the survey progressed, it revealed post-Conquest activities at the site visible in surface concentrations of artifacts that were clearly not pre-Columbian, but did not look contemporary, as well as non-indigenous citrus and palm trees. They are represented on the site map by a circle bisected horizontally by a straight line. Early explorers, chicle gatherers who tapped the sapodilla trees for the sap from which to make chewing gum, the occasional tourist, and a small settlement near the Tikal Aguada (waterhole) (Figs. 4, L07, L08) that came and went towards the end of the 19th century had all left their material traces. Tikal, although abandoned and isolated, had been drawing attention to itself ever since its official discovery in 1848.

Tikal Project investigations into historic activities were of a haphazard character. Pottery vessels and other artifacts were collected in the course of other activities such as survey and excavation, and were brought into the field laboratory to be cleaned, repaired, and catalogued. As this late material accumulated, some of the Project's members became interested in discovering more about its origins, particularly how it related to a small settlement, or *aldea,* reported to have existed at Tikal in the late 19th century. In 1962 we planned to do a controlled excavation of RS 5F-1, the only house in the aldea that had stone wall footings (Fig. 3; Palka 2005: fig. 6.29), but it could not be carried out until the following field season. In 1963 RS 5F-1

was cleared, trenched, and recorded. Unlike most of the residences of the pre-Columbian city, the pole and thatch homes of the 19th-century settlers were built directly on the ground surface without raised platforms (cf., TR. 19, 21). Furthermore, because abandoned structures in the Petén built with traditional methods and local materials (e.g., Figs. L09-L14) will disintegrate completely within a few decades, the residences of the aldea, with the notable exception of RS 5F-1, could only be identified by the artifacts, hearths, and exotic trees associated with them.

Eventually the question arose of what we should do with the information we had gathered. The original, more creative plan was to publish the archaeological finds in an ethnohistoric context. I would report on the archaeology and Rubén E. Reina would present the ethnohistory (TR. 12:59). However, this collaboration did not come to pass, and so the focus of the report was reduced to a presentation of the historic archaeological remains with only minimal cultural background. The materials are reported as scattered finds and as Recent Sites (RS), a term borrowed from geology to distinguish later activities from those of the great pre-Columbian city.

Tikal After the Conquest

The best-documented events are mentioned here; a more complete list is presented in Appendix E. The first European to mention Tikal may have been Fr. Andrés de Avendaño y Loyola, a Franciscan priest, who made two trips to the Petén at the end of the 17th century (Avendaño 1987). On his second trip, as he and a small party of men tried to make their way to

Tipu in Yucatan, they were abandoned in the forest by their guide. For days they wandered lost through the region north of Lake Petén Itzá and nearly starved to death before reaching safety (Jones 1998:219). Avendaño describes seeing "old buildings" during their wanderings:

> Among these high hills which we passed over there is a variety of old buildings, excepting some in which I recognized apartments, and though they were very high and my strength was little, I climbed up them (though with trouble). They were in the form of a convent, with the small cloisters and many living rooms all roofed over and arched like a wagon, and whitened inside with plaster, which is very abundant throughout that region, since all the ridges are composed of it. These buildings consequently do not resemble those which are here in this Province, for the latter are of pure worked stone, laid without mortar, particularly the part which relates to arches, but the former are of rough stone and mortar covered with plaster.
>
> It seemed to us that these buildings stood near a settlement, from the information the soldiers had given us, when we were going on the new road to Guatemala, but it turned out to be the dream of a blind man, since we found ourselves, as we saw afterwards, very far from a settlement. (Avendaño 1987:61–62)

This is a rather sketchy description and the area north of the Lake includes more than one pre-Columbian site that has masonry buildings with plastered walls. Nevertheless, Sylvanus G. Morley was convinced that Avendaño could only have seen Tikal (1938:55), and his opinion has been generally accepted.

The name of a hamlet called Tikal is briefly mentioned again in 1698, during the chaotic times after Martin de Ursua's conquest of the Itzas the previous year. This settlement was two days' journey directly northeast of the town of Ketz on the north shore of Lake Petén Itzá (Jones 1998:350). However, none of the Historic materials we gathered appeared to be as old as the late 17th century. After the mention of the Tikal hamlet, there is a long documentary hiatus until 1848.

Despite the difficulties in reaching Tikal before the construction of the airfield in 1951, and the oft-mentioned problem of obtaining drinking water, there is an impressive number of *published* visits to the site after its discovery in 1848 (Appendix E). Ambrosio Tut, the Governor of Petén, and Colonel Modesto Méndez (Fig. L15), the Corregidor of the Petén (Méndez 1955), are credited with the official discovery of Tikal. In February of 1848 Tut and Méndez spent six days exploring the ruins, and Méndez made another visit to the ruins in 1852 (Hammond 1987).

Accounts of visits by Bernoulli, Valenzuela, Maudslay, and Maler mention the 19th-century Tikal aldea, which is the source of most of the material culture reported in this volume. The earliest-known written mention of the aldea by travelers may be in a letter that the Swiss physician and explorer Carl Gustav Bernoulli (Fig. L16) addressed to the Austrian explorer Teobert Maler (Fig. L17), on October 22, 1877 (Meyer-Holdampf 1997:105). Maler reports that: "He wrote that he had succeeded in visiting Tikal in the neighborhood of which, near the aguada, a few Indian families were still living" (1911:42).

Bernoulli was from Basle. He arranged for the removal of the magnificent carved wooden lintels of Str. 5D-4 (Temple IV) (TR. 33A:101; Appendix K:171) to the ethnographic museum of his home town, the Museum der Kulturen. But Bernoulli never saw the lintels again. He died in San Francisco on his return voyage at the age of 44.

In 1879, or shortly before, the Ministry of Development of the Guatemalan Government sent an Inspector of Agriculture on a tour of the Petén. This official, Salvador Valenzuela, spent four days at Tikal and included a brief description of the ruins and the Tikal aldea in his report of 1879 (Appendix K; Valenzuela 1951:408–10). At that time the aldea was composed of ten families, three of Lacandon and seven of Yucatecan natives, but Valenzuela says little else about it.

By 1881, however, on the first of two visits by the English explorer Alfred P. Maudslay (Fig. L18), the Tikal aldea had been abandoned (Maudslay 1889–1902:44–50). Maudslay's second visit took place the next year. He made two observations that pertain to the settlement:

> The place is absolutely desolate, the nearest Indian village being San Andrés and some other

small hamlets on the borders of the lake [Petén Itzá]. (1889–1902:44)

A few years before the date of my visit to Tikal a party of Indians from the borders of the lake had attempted to form a settlement in the neighborhood of the ruins. The solitary survivor of this party accompanied me as a guide, all the others having died of fever. (1889–1902:49)

Even though Maudslay stayed less than a week on each visit (Graham 2002:90, 107; Morley 1938:267), he published a good description of the site well illustrated with photographs, including two of special interest to this Report, his camp and that of his workmen (1889–1902: pl. 80a, b; Maudslay and Maudslay 1899). Maudslay's workmen camped in the forest (Fig. 8), while Maudslay set up house in the rear gallery (Figs. 9, 10) of the fourth story of the masonry range structure designated as Str. 5D-52 on the Tikal Map, and as RS 5D-2 in this Report (Fig. 2e). Although the outer range of rooms in this Late Classic structure have fallen away (Fig. L19), the inner gallery where Maudslay stayed was still well preserved in the 1960s and a pleasant place from which to enjoy the view over the Palace Reservoir to Str. 5D-5, Great Temple V. Some years later, Teobert Maler photographed the now-empty gallery in which Maudslay had resided (Figs. 11, 12).

Maler, who made two visits to Tikal in 1895 and 1904, deplored the amount of damage done to the pre-Columbian site. Some of it he attributed to chicleros (Maler 1911:9), but he placed most of the blame on the decamped Tikal settlers (1908:119; 1911:28, 29, 33). Maler claims they were encouraged in their depredations by "treasurer seekers from Petén Itzá," and it is a sad fact that the best-preserved carved lintels of zapote wood had already been carried off before the time of Maler's second visit in 1904. The fires set by the settlers to prepare their cornfields (cf. L20) had also cracked and calcined the stone monuments on the Great Plaza.

Maler spent more time at Tikal than any other explorer before him; eight days in 1895 and a little over three months in 1904. Each time he was accompanied by a fairly large party of men who brought tools, cooking utensils, and personal effects with them. Like Maudslay, Maler also camped out on the Central Acropolis, in the center first-story room of the north-

ern gallery of the large, well-preserved range structure now designated as Str. 5D-65 on the Tikal Map and RS 5D-1 here (Figs. 11, L21-L23). This stucture is about 50 m west of the one in which Maudslay lived. Maler named the building in which he stayed The Palace of the Two Stories and the building in which Maudslay stayed The Palace of the Five Stories. Clearing of Str. 5D-65 in 1958 produced a pottery pitcher and a reworked pottery water jar, RS 5D-1 (Fig. 26c, d), which may pertain to Maler's visits.

Men from the village of San José on Lake Petén Itzá, about 25 miles south-southwest of Tikal (Fig. 1), were included among the workers on both of Maler's expeditions. In 1904 men from San Andrés, the village nearest to San José, were also present. The men from the Lake camped out about 450 m southeast of Maler's residence. They established themselves in Structure Group 5E-11, near Str. 5E-58 and 5E-60, which Maler designated as The Palace of the Façades with the Vertical Grooves (Fig. 2f). Although some survey and excavation were carried out in Group 5E-11 in the 1960s (Orrego and Larios 1983), no Recent materials were reported. A few men from Tenosique, Tabasco, were on Maler's 1904 trip and stayed close to Maler on the Central Acropolis.

In June, 1901, Professor Walter M. Wolfe of Brigham Young University and Brigham Young High School (Fig. L24) spent three, apparently excruciatingly uncomfortable days at Tikal (Appendix I). He reported making a test excavation into a temple, which quite probably was into the roofcomb of Str. 5D-3 (Great Temple III) (Figs. 6, 7).

The chicle extraction industry in the Petén got underway in the 1890s. Until a synthetic substitute was invented in the 1940s, chicle, the sap of the sapodilla tree (*Manikara zapota*), also referred to in Spanish as *chicozapote* and *chico sapote,* formed the base for chewing gum. The industry enjoyed a spurt of rapid growth during World War I and another during World War II, held steady from the late 1940s into the 1970s, and went into decline after that (Schwartz 1990: Table 4.2). Sapodilla trees prefer somewhat elevated ground and are often found near ancient Maya ruins. Chicleros have been passing through Tikal since the early years of the 20th century, and at least one probable campsite, RS 4B-1, contributes to the remains of Historic Tikal. Perhaps this campsite resembled the camp of Maudslay's workmen (Fig. 8).

During the late 1950s and 1960s, Rubén E. Reina of the University of Pennsylvania made an ethnographic study of the villages around Lake Petén Itzá (Figs. 1, L25-L28; TR. 10; Reina 1962, 1967, 1977; Reina and Hill 1978), and the Tikal Project became a grateful beneficiary of some of the results of his research, as well as a small study collection of pottery vessels from San José Petén (cf. Fig. 14).

In the course of his ethnographic research Reina discovered in the archives of the village of San José census documents of the period 1876–1878, which include records for a small settlement at Tikal. At some time before 1876, the Tikal settlement was organized as an aldea under the jurisdiction of the village of San José (Reina 1977:7–8). Reina notes that the 1876 census lists 20 males and 22 females organized in 15 families (houses), the 1877 census reports 2 male and 4 female Ladinos (of non-indigenous culture) among an unspecified population total, and the 1878 census gives 22 adults and 17 children in 15 families. By the time of Valenzuela's visit, the number of families had dwindled to 10, and by the time of Maudslay's first visit in 1881 no one was left. Through a comparison of family surnames in the Tikal and San José censuses, Reina established population movement between the two settlements.

Teobert Maler, who seemed to take an interest in everything, had the most to say about the settlement at Tikal. He states (1911:24) that the settlers were one of several bands of Yucatecans who fled south into the Petén during the bitter and prolonged War of the Castes that ravaged the northern part of the Yucatán Peninsula from 1847 to about 1870 (Reed 1964). He goes on to excoriate the settlers for vandalism, saying they were encouraged by a Colonel Méndez, who may even have brought in looters from San José and San Andrés on the Lake (Maler 1911:49–50). Maler says that the only trace these people left behind them were numerous lemon (that is, lime) and bitter orange trees between Str. 5E-58 and 5E-60, where Maler's men camped, and around the Tikal Aguada. In addition to the fruit trees, the settlers grew maize in the Great Plaza by slash-and-burn methods (swidden), which may account for the calcined condition of some of the ancient stone monuments, as well as smaller stone artifacts from surface contexts.

The cause of the abandonment of the Tikal aldea remains unclear. Maler has the following to say:

But in the course of time the great distance from other settlements grew irksome to the colony and the settlers gradually dispersed in different directions. The Peteneros, however, ascribe the breaking up of the colony to a plague of bats. (1911:33)

In 1958, Reina was also told the story of the plague of bats, and also one of a plague of mosquitoes, and rats that ate up the corn (TR. 10:220). Another likely cause of abandonment of the Tikal aldea could well have been the difficulties of growing maize there by swidden methods (Reina 1967). Violence may also have been involved, as hinted by Walter Wolfe's observation that in 1879 Guatemalan soldiers were sent to Tikal against the Indians living there (Walter M. Wolfe 1901g; Appendix I). When the aldea was finally abandoned, at least some of the Tikal settlers moved to San José. As late as 1958 an elderly woman living in San José was said to have been born at Tikal.

Migration from Petén to Socotz in what is now Belize is noted by Cowgill (1963:505), who speaks of some degree of depopulation in the late 19th century due to an economic depression. Throughout his report of 1908, which covers his activities in 1904 and 1905, Maler remarks on the continuing depopulation of the Petén.

His accounts support the information from others that, in fact, several groups of Yucatecan fugitives established temporary settlements in the forests of the Petén. Maler speaks of families of "free Maya," living in Quintana Roo and the Petén around the middle of the 19th century, but which were gone by his time. Such a settlement existed at the ancient Maya ruins of Naranjo in the Petén close to the border of British Honduras:

Inquiring of the older people in Benque Viejo [now Melchor de Mencos] what name this tract bore before the chicleros visited, I learned that in the middle of the nineteenth century a few Indian or half-African families had settled there near the large aguada, and among other things had planted some orange trees around their cabins. Hence this settlement was called "El Naranjo" or "El Naranjal." These people must be credited with doing no harm to the ruins—in contrast to the band of vandals which destroyed Tikal. (Maler 1908:119)

Later the Naranjo settlement was abandoned and the people are said to have moved to British Honduras.

In 1998, the Lacandon Archaeological Project (LAP) directed by Joel W. Palka of the University of Illinois at Chicago carried out excavations at and around some of the Recent Sites in the southern part of the 19th-century aldea, which had been recorded over thirty years earlier by the Tikal Project (Figs. 2h, 3, L29-L45). Palka gave the name La Palmera to that part of the aldea he investigated (2005:154). One of his research objectives was to look for Lacandon material culture among the recovered remains, but no artifacts characteristic of the 19th-century Lacandon could be identified (2005:168, 191–92).

Palka discovered that metal detectors were an efficient way of locating house sites in the rainforest (Fig. L46). His metal detector survey and excavations produced a sample of portable material culture, which adds to the inventory of artifacts published in this volume. The two artifact collections—the one made by the Tikal Project and the one made by the Lacandon Archaeological Project—are complementary samples of the same archaeological context. The Tikal Project was able to recover previously undisturbed surface finds, which included complete examples of larger artifact types such as stone manos and metates, glass bottles, and pottery vessels. The sample of material culture recovered by the La Palmera excavations lacks complete examples of large artifacts, but includes a greater variety of smaller ones, especially artifacts of metal, as well as many more animal bones.

Comment on Tikal Recent Sites

Archaeologically, the existence of the Tikal aldea is well established by surface concentrations and scattered finds of Historic artifacts, particularly in the vicinity of the Tikal Aguada. Some of the finds seem more properly attributed to explorers, and to chicleros whose activities in the Tikal area mushroomed from small beginnings in the 1890s to a high level of production in the 1920s (Schwartz 1990:29) before declining in the 1970s. However, the presence of many pottery vessels, hearths, the remains of a structure with stone wall footings, exotic palm trees, and relict orange groves (Appendices F and G; Figs. L31,

L32), indicates that some concentrations of artifacts belong to a settlement more permanent than the kind usually made by explorers or chicle gatherers.

The settlement pattern and material culture show that the 19th-century residents lived like other small communities of semi-acculturated indigenous agriculturalists of Mesoamerica. They shared the same basic complex of cultural traits presumably established shortly after the Conquest that has survived to varying degrees in the more remote parts of the region. Documented administrative, economic, and social ties, as well as items of material culture (Appendix H), connected the Tikal aldea to the village of San José on Lake Petén Itzá. A few items of material culture hint at connections of some kind to Yucatán and ultimately to the United States (e.g., Appendix J).

At present, the beginning and the end of the Tikal aldea are still obscure. At some time in the late 19th century, a few families established themselves near the Tikal Aguada. They were probably one of a number of such groups who sought refuge in the forests of the Petén from the upheavals brought about by the War of the Castes in Yucatán. By 1876 the settlement had become an aldea of the town of San José Petén. Documentation exists for the occupation of the aldea into the year 1879. But by 1881 it had been abandoned. Ethnographic research suggests that when the aldea was abandoned, most of its residents moved to San José.

Available data are also ambiguous regarding the nature of the aldea's abandonment. The quantity, variety, condition, and quality of the associated portable material culture suggest that it was abandoned on short notice. Palka notes that no effort was made to cache or store small usable items and, furthermore, that the settlers did not plan to return (Joel Palka, pers. comm. 2009). Besides the still usable, imported manufactured goods, such as the glass bottles and metal artifacts, there are also the citrus trees and exotic palms to consider. At least eight of the aldea sites were associated with planted, not native trees. At Tikal, an orange tree needs at least five years' growth before it will start to produce fruit (C.L. Lundell, pers. comm. 1962), which, in turn, may indicate that the Tikal settlers intended to stay longer than the length of time documented by available written sources. Arguing against a hurried departure, however, is the apparent absence of a local oral tradition about it or any clear signs of violence.

The oral history of San José does give plagues of fever, mosquitoes, bats, and rats as reasons for abandonment. Palka (2005:116–17) mentions diseases such as smallpox, yellow fever, malaria, and influenza as a serious problem in the area. There was also a good deal of violence (2005:121–22). Petén settlers feared "wild" Indians, referred to as *huites*, who occasionally raided their settlements, particularly those along the north shore of Lake Petén. During the 1860s a garrison of 40 soldiers was stationed in the town of San Andrés (Soza 1970:257) to cope with this problem. Walter M. Wolfe tantalizingly notes that soldiers had been sent to Tikal "against the Indians" in 1879 (Appendix I), which might be supported by the occurrence of a bayonet of a type used in the 19th century (Appendix F). Valenzuela does not mention such an event in his Report dated 1 June 1879 (Appendix K), which suggests that it occurred after his visit and may have been connected to the disap-pearance of the settlement. But, in the end, we also cannot discount Maler's observation that the aldea was abandoned because of the practical difficulties of trying to maintain daily existence in such an isolated place (1911:33).

The Organization of This Report

Chapter 2 presents an overview of settlement pattern and scattered finds, as well as a brief description of each Recent Site. The Tikal Project's collection of Historic artifacts and pottery is described in Chapter 3. The variables used for describing items of material culture are the same as those used in TR. 27, Parts A and B, which report on the artifacts of Tikal, and are presented in Appendices A-D on the CD-ROM accompanying this Report. No burials, caches, or problematical deposits were defined for Historic Tikal.

Settlement Pattern and Scattered Finds

Historic materials occurred as scattered finds of one or more objects or as concentrations of materials that suggested now-vanished residences. Finds of more than one object were designated Recent Sites and numbered according to the map squares in which they were found in the same manner as pre-Columbian features (TR. 5:6). Fifteen Recent Sites were defined (Table 2.1). Two Recent Sites, RS 5D-1 and RS 5D-2, were found within rooms of still-standing ancient architecture on Tikal's Central Acropolis, Gp. 5D-11 (Fig. 2e).

According to artifact content and deposition, 11 of 15 defined Recent Sites pertain to the 19th-century Tikal aldea (Fig. 2g, h) or were contemporary with it (Fig. 2a, i), 2 are attributed to the explorers Maudslay and Maler (Fig. 2e), while 1 is a probable chiclero camp (Fig. 2c). One, RS 5F-5, has subsequently been reclassified because the associated materials appear to be entirely pre-Columbian.

Referring to Table 2.2, the following observations can be made:

Most of the archaeological features and associated material culture of the Tikal aldea are also characteristic of somewhat acculturated Maya-speaking settlements of the 19th and early 20th centuries, for example, the X-Cacal indigenes of Quintana Roo (Villa Rojas 1945:53), San Pedro la Laguna on Lake Atitlán (Paul 1941), Yucatán (Redfield and Villa Rojas 1934), and especially San José Petén (Appendix H; Figs. 14, L25–28; TR. 10; Reina 1962).

Among features, hearths assembled of three or more large stones or cut masonry blocks salvaged from the ruins found with RS 4B-1, RS 5F-1, 5F-2, 5F-3, and 5F-4 were common throughout Mesoamerica. At Tikal it was possible to trace the walls

of only one house, at RS 5F-1, and in this case the hearth was within the residence at its western end (Fig. 15:7). This accords with native rather than Ladino custom, where the kitchen is usually a separate structure (e.g., Palka 2005; Schwartz 1990). Villa Rojas reported interior hearths in Quintana Roo (Villa Rojas 1945:52).

Before the mid-1950s, most of the travelers who succeeded in reaching the site depended upon the Tikal Aguada in Map Sq 4F for water (Fig. 4), even though nearly everyone complained about the quality of the water and Morley stated that it sometimes dried up in April (1938:269). In this connection it is interesting to note that glass bottles or pottery water jars were found at both of the explorers' sites and all but two of the aldea sites. Edwin Shook recalled that visitors from the Carnegie Institution of Washington relied for water on the Aguada Corriental, ca. 1.5 km to the south-southwest of the Tikal Aguada (Fig. 2i). The presence of a hand mill, machete fragment, and a lime tree at Corriental suggested that a residence of some kind had been established near it (William Haviland, pers. comm. 2007). This cluster was designated RS 7E-1. The chiclero camp, RS 4B-1 (Fig. 2c), probably drew water from the nearby Aguada Subín. I could not determine a source of water for RS 2G-1, situated on the peripheries (Fig. 2a).

The settlers salvaged and made extensive use of pre-Columbian Maya stone artifacts: chert bifaces, flakes, and hammerstones (Figs. L39, L40), obsidian blades, jadeite celts, limestone rubbing stones, and whole and fragmentary manos and pieces of metates. These reused artifacts are described and illustrated in TR. 27, Parts A and B. The settlers also fashioned manos and metates from carved and plain monuments (Fig. 18–21c). They used iron or steel tools that left distinctive marks on the stone. The intensive use made of salvaged artifacts suggests it was not easy for the settlers at Tikal to obtain goods from elsewhere.

Settlement Pattern and Architecture

With the exception of the apparent outliers, RS 2G-1 and 7E-1, recorded sites of the Tikal aldea form two groups in Map Squares 4F and 5F (Fig. 2g, h). Maler remarked that a favored location for the settlers' *milpas* (cornfields) was the area between the Great Plaza westwards to Str. 5D-3, Great Temple III in Map Square 5D (Fig. 1).

The complete disappearance of the aldea's houses, except for RS 5F-1, suggests that they were constructed with local materials and construction methods with walls of poles set vertically, roofs of thatch palm (called *guano*, probably *Sabal morrisiana*), and floors of hard-packed earth (cf. Figs. L09-L14). Stones had been laid around the exterior of the pole walls of the structure at RS 5F-1 (Figs. 15, 16, L34-L35; Palka 2005: fig. 6.29), which enabled us to trace its plan. The stone perimeter, off-center doorway, dirt floor, and pole walls are characteristic of modern San José houses, but the plan of the RS 5F-1 structure is oblong, while San José houses are oblong with one rounded end. Another difference is that the hearth of the Tikal house was within the walls, while in San José the hearth is in a separate kitchen structure (Fig. L27), an arrangement that often occurs in contemporary tropical Mesoamerica. Unfortunately, the absence of wall remains makes it impossible to determine where the hearths in the other Tikal houses were located, e.g., at RS 5F-2 (Figs. 17, L36). At some sites, no hearth was observed.

The hearths at four Recent Sites where we have this information consisted of three or more large stones, a type once standard throughout the area (Redfield and Villa Rojas 1934:35; Villa Rojas 1945:53), although no longer used, for example, in San José. The stones used for the hearth at RS 5F-1 are large chunks of bedrock, and this may also have been the case at RS 5F-4 and at the chiclero camp at RS 4B-1. On the other hand, the hearth of RS 5F-2 was made of cut stone blocks (Figs. 17, L36). These

were left in situ and I was unable to examine them. These blocks might have been taken from ancient buildings or even from plain stone monuments. Some of the larger stone blocks found at Recent Sites could have served as seats and tables (Joel Palka, pers. comm. 1999).

In 1998 Palka excavated 8 house sites, as Operations 1–8, at La Palmera, which constitute the southern cluster of the Tikal aldea (Palka 2005:151–62). A concordance with Tikal Project collections is given in Table 2.3 (TR. 11; Palka 2005: Map 6.4). LAP Operations 1, 4, and 8 investigated residences that were not recorded by the Tikal Project. Operations 2 and 3 excavated RS 5F-3 and determined that it probably included 2 houses. Operations 5 and 6 excavated RS 5F-2, and Operation 7 investigated RS 5F-1. LAP excavations have added at least 4 more residences to the 10 previously recorded by the Tikal Project. This brings the total to 14 houses, which is close to the figure of 15 families mentioned in the 1876 and 1878 San José censuses (Reina 1977).

Description of Recent Sites

On the figure references, L figures are in Appendix L on the accompanying CD-ROM. 27A: refers to TR. 27, Part A, 27B: to TR. 27, Part B, and 33A: to TR. 33, Part A. The Historic artifacts are listed by catalogue or lot number in Appendix D on the CD-ROM.

Recent Site 2G-1, Lot 1D/11
(Fig. 2a)

Tikal Map location: 2G 58S 320E. Collected February 17, 1960, by Hans M. Gregersen and his team of surveyors.

Objects were scattered over a fairly large area, approximately 10 by 14 m. No hearth was observed.

ASSOCIATED MATERIAL
Recent
Slab metate, 1D-51/11 (Fig. 19)
2 glass bottles, 1D-55a, b/11 (Fig. 22c, d)
Iron or steel pillbox, 1D-54/11 (Fig. 23c)
Iron or steel axe head, 1D-53/11 (Fig. 23g)

Indented-fillet pottery bowl, 1D-45/11 (Fig. 26h)

Small pottery bowl, 1D-46/11 (Fig. 27e)

Large pottery bowl with everted rim, 1D-47/11 (Fig. 28f)

2 incomplete large bowls with everted rims, 1D-49/11, 1D-50/11

Side of a pottery jar, 1D-48/11

Pre-Columbian

Chert ovate biface, complete, reused as a hammer, 1D-52/11 (Fig. 27B:7a)

COMMENT

RS 2G-1 is unusual for its isolated position, relatively large proportion of unbroken artifacts, and our present uncertainty as to its source of water. The artifacts suggest its occupation was contemporary with that of the Tikal aldea.

Recent Site 4B-1, Lot 1D/10
(Fig. 2c)

Map location: 4B 421S 23E. Collected March 27, 1958, by Richard Wurman.

ASSOCIATED MATERIAL

Recent

Graduated glass bottle, 1D-39/10 (Fig. 22i)

Large pottery bowl with everted rim, 1D-38/10 (Fig. 28d)

COMMENT

Wurman noted that there were "many fireplaces of 3 and 4 stones" (1958:14). The few people who have seen this isolated site identified it as a probable chiclero camp. The glass bottle looks fairly new and the large bowl is of a type that was still made and used in San José in the early 1960s (Fig. L27). The probable source of water for RS 4B-1 was the nearby Aguada Subín.

Recent Site 4F-1, Lot 1D/2
(Fig. 2g)

Map location: 4F 267S 311E. Collected in 1956 by Antonio Ortiz and Gregorio Ibarra.

ASSOCIATED MATERIAL

Recent

Complete pottery jar, 1D-13/2 (Fig. 27b)

Incomplete pottery jar, 1D-13b/2

COMMENT

The two water jars found near the northwest corner of the Tikal Aguada suggest incidental debris rather than a living site.

Recent Site 4F-2, Lot 1D/9
(Fig. 2g)

Map location: 4F 172S 236E, off the northwest corner of the Posada de la Selva hotel. Collected on February 21, 1958, by Vivian Broman.

ASSOCIATED MATERIAL

Recent

Glass wine bottle, 1D-58/9 (Fig. 22e)

Pottery baking dish rim fragments, 1D-67/9 (Fig. 26b)

Small pottery jar, incomplete, 1D-64/9 (Fig. 27d)

Small pottery bowl, incomplete, 1D-60/9 (Fig. 27g)

Pottery bowl rim, 1D-65/9 (Fig. 28h)

Small pottery ringstand bowl, incomplete, 1D-66/9 (Fig. 28i)

4 large pottery bowls with everted rims, incomplete, 1D-59/9, 1D-61/9 through 63/9

Large pottery bowl base, heavily burned, possibly reused as a griddle, 1D-68/9

Several scattered bitter orange trees, *Citrus aurantium* L.

Pre-Columbian

Chert flake core, battered, used as a hammerstone, 1D/9

Plano-convex limestone mano end and edge fragment, 1D-69/9

Pottery panpipe mouthpiece fragment, 1D-79/9

COMMENT

RS 4F-2 covers a large area, which suggests that more than one house stood here. Broman notes that the material was distributed in seven small concentrations over an area of ca. 12.5 by 9.0 m. Two "grinding stones," not collected, were also associated with this site.

Recent Site 4F-3, Lot 1D/1
(Fig. 2g)

Map location: 4F 185S 286E near the Tikal Aguada, but not shown on the Tikal Map. Collected December 15, 1956, by Edwin M. Shook.

ASSOCIATED MATERIAL
Recent
Tripod metate, 1D-28/1 (Fig. 18h)
Slab metate, 1D-4/1 (Fig. 21e)
Large pottery bowl with vertical lug handles, incomplete, 1D-57/1 (Fig. 28b)
3 large pottery bowls with everted rims, incomplete, 1D-23/1, 1D-24a, b/1
Sherds of one or more jars, 1D-25/1
About a dozen bitter orange trees, *Citrus aurantium*
At least one lime tree, *Citrus aurantifolia*

Pre-Columbian
Quartzite mano midsection fragment with rectangular cross section used as a hammer, 1D-2/1
3 small fragments of turtleback metates, 1 of granite, 1D-3/1, and 2 of quartzite, 1D-5/1 and 1D-6/1
Fragment of grooved, weathered white plaster, 1D-1/1 (Fig. 27B:151c)
About 50 pre-Columbian sherds, including several of the Late Classic Imix ceramic complex (TR. 25A)

COMMENT
The material was found scattered along the top of the rise north of and parallel to the Tikal Aguada where the Tikal Project camp was established in 1956. The presence of the metates and pottery vessels suggests one or more houses, but no data regarding distribution were collected.

Recent Site 4F-4, Lots 1A/1 and 1D/4
(Fig. 2g)

Map location: not located on the Tikal Map. Collected in 1956 and 1957 by workmen who built the Tikal Project camp along the northern embankment of the Tikal Aguada.

ASSOCIATED MATERIAL
End fragment of a large limestone artifact of unknown

use, 1A-1/1 (Fig. 21d)
Glass bottle, 1D-8a/4 (Fig. 22b)
Glass bottle, 1D-8b/4 (Fig. 22h)
Pottery pitcher, 1D-9/4 (Fig. 26e)
Large pottery bowl with everted rim, 1D-10/4 (Fig. 28e)
Bitter orange trees mentioned in connection with RS 4F-3

COMMENT
RS 4F-4 includes material without exact provenience found on and around the Tikal Aguada embankment.

Recent Site 4F-5, Lot 1D/9A
(Fig. 2g)

Collected in October 1958 by Antonio Ortiz's workmen during the construction of the Posada de la Selva hotel. It is not shown on the site map.

ASSOCIATED MATERIAL
Recent
Iron tripod cooking pot, 1D-70/9A (Fig. 22l)
Pottery pitcher base, burned, 1D-71/9A
Pottery ringstand bowl, 1D-72/9A (Fig. 28g)
Scattered bitter orange trees, *Citrus aurantium* L.

Pre-Columbian
Midsection fragment of a thin biface of fine dark chert, 1D-77/9A
Tip fragment of a crude thin biface of gray obsidian, 1D-43/9A
Head of a small minor sculpture of limestone, 1D-74/9A (Fig. 27A:238f)
1 complete, 1D-73a/9A, and 3 fragmentary, 1D-42/9A, 1D-73b, c/9A, jadeite celts (Fig. 27B:99i) reused as polishing stones
Heavily patinated elongate nodule of fine dark chert used as a polishing stone, 1D-41/9A (Fig. 27B:93g)
Flat piece of cut marine shell incised with a delicate two-glyph inscription, 1D-44/9A, Miscellaneous Text 362 (Fig. 27A:181d)
Fragment of a weathered, large, hollow, moldmade pottery figurine of woman in a style unknown at Tikal, 1D-40/9A (Fig. 26a)

Weathered fragment of a moldmade pottery whistle representing two human beings, 1D-76/9A

Unperforated worked sherd disk with ground perimeter, 1D-75/9A (Fig. 27B:135e)

COMMENT

Data on the distribution of artifacts were not recorded. However, the types represented suggest that the large hollow figurine, minor sculpture head, and shell artifact may have come from elsewhere. The unusual concentration of jadeite celts and fragments, worked sherd disk, and the highly polished chert nodule suggest a locus for pottery production.

Recent Site 5D-1, Lot 15B/2 (Figs. 2e, 13, L21-L23)

Map location: Room 8 of Str. 5D-65 of Gp. 5D-11, the Central Acropolis. Collected June 9–10, 1958, by Richard E.W. Adams.

ASSOCIATED MATERIAL
Recent

Base of a small pottery water jar converted into a bowl, 15B-2/2 (Fig. 26c)

Pottery pitcher, 15B-1/2 (Fig. 26d)

COMMENT

Teobert Maler lived in this structure during his expeditions of 1895 and 1904, so perhaps the two pottery vessels pertain to his time there. The pitcher and water jar forms were still made in San José Petén in the late 1950s-early 1960s.

Recent Site 5D-2, Lots 44A/3, 44A/11 (Figs. 2e, 9–12, L19)

Map location: Second story north gallery of Str. 5D-52 in Gp. 5D-11, the Central Acropolis. Collected March 1–8, 1962, by Robert H. Dyson.

ASSOCIATED MATERIAL
Recent

Iron or steel chisel, 44A-34/11 (Fig. 25a)

Two loop handles from a pottery jar, 44A-30a, b/3

COMMENT

Maudslay camped in Str. 5D-52 on the two occasions he visited Tikal in 1881 and 1882. The jar handles were found in the gallery where Maudslay stayed. The chisel comes from the surface of the northeast room of the north gallery on the first story of Str. 5D-52. This gallery is below the one occupied by Maudslay.

Recent Site 5F-1, Lots 1D/6, 34A/1–14 (Figs. 2h, 3, 15, 16, L33–L35)

Map location: 5F S320 E56, overlying pre-Columbian Gp. 5F-5. The site was first collected as lot 1D/6 by Vivian Broman and Edwin M. Shook in May 1957 and excavated as Operation 34A, lots 1–14, under my direction in February 1963. In 1998 additional excavations were carried out as Operation 7 by the LAP (Table 2.3; Palka 2005: Map 6.4, fig. 6.29).

RS 5F-1 consisted of the remains of a house and a grove of orange trees of undetermined extent that surrounded the structure on all sides. A coconut palm found ca. 12 m to the north of the house by Dennis Puleston (Appendix G; Fig. L47) may also have been associated with it. In 1957 James Hazard (1957:42) and Shook reported surface concentrations of large stone fragments or outcrops about 60 m to the northwest of RS 5F-1. However, I was unable to locate them in 1963 or in 1964.

The structure was large, with maximum dimensions of 9.25 x 4.75 m, oriented approximately east-west. There was one entrance, facing south, slightly off-center towards the west. The structure was partially built over the edge of an ancient platform lying between Str. 5F-27 and 5F-28 of Gp. 5F-5. A surface collection comprising a complete metate and two incomplete pottery bowls with everted rims, all of Recent types, was made in 1957 at a point approximately 3.15 m north of the structure's northern wall foundation.

At present this structure is the only one with stone wall footings associated with the Tikal aldea, which suggests that it had an important civic or religious function. Although Recent Sites tend to be scattered, three lie within a radius of 140 m of RS 5F-1. These are RS 5F-2, 5F-3, and 5F-4, described below.

EXCAVATION

In 1963 excavations were undertaken in the structure at RS 5F-1 to determine its function (Moholy-Nagy 1963). The ground within the boundaries of the stone foundations was cleared to the level of the floor. Because the floor consisted of packed earth, it was defined by the artifacts we assumed were resting upon it. An unexpected discovery was an interior three-stone hearth at the western end of the building.

After the floor of the structure had been cleared, a transverse trench was begun on the south side through the doorway and carried northwards across the structure and through the opposite wall. The trench was first carried down to the surface of the pre-Columbian platform, and then approximately 30 cm farther into the platform's fill. Another trench ran west from the eastern retaining wall of the building to meet the transverse north-south trench. This trench disclosed a large, oblong patch of white plaster at floor level. Finally the hearth was removed and a test pit was excavated to a depth of ca. 35 cm below the level of the floor into the floor fill.

The pre-Columbian platform had at least one descending step going from east to west (Fig. 16). The fill consisted of large, irregular blocks of the local bedrock. The ca. 70 sherds recovered from the fill were all pre-Columbian and dated from the Late Preclassic to the middle of the Late Classic period (T. Patrick Culbert, pers. comm. 1963), indicating that the platform had been built sometime after the appearance of the Imix Ceramic Complex (ca. A.D. 700–870).

TIME SPANS AND ASSOCIATED MATERIAL

Excavations suggested three time-spans for the RS 5F-1 structure.

TIME-SPAN 3

The construction of the Recent building (lots 34A/3, 4, 6, 8, 10, 11, 14, most of lot 34A/9, and part of lot 34A/13).

A heavy deposit of black earth behind the eastern foundation of the structure and the irregular surface of the pre-Columbian platform indicate that the platform was ruined and overgrown at the time of the construction of the building.

Nothing remained of the walls of the Recent structure other than the foundation perimeter of rough chunks of bedrock somewhat smaller than those used for the ancient platform. Since the dirt floor seemed to be firmer and better preserved near the stones and turned up to them in some places, the walls may have been of mud-plastered vertical poles, perhaps the same kind of construction common in the Petén today (cf. Fig. L27). The stones were laid along the exterior of the mud and pole house wall. At the eastern end of the structure, the stones also served as a retaining wall. No traces of mortar were found, nor were postholes observed.

A great deal of material had been filled into the eastern end of the stone perimeter. The sherds and artifacts included in this floor fill suggest the neighboring pre-Columbian structures 5F-27 and 5F-28 as probable sources. About 450 sherds were recovered. Recognizable types pertained to the Manik, Ik, and Imix Ceramic Complexes, i.e., the Early, Early Late, and Late Late Classic periods (T. Patrick Culbert, pers. comm. 1963). Two small sherds, a metal button, and a fragment of a metal box strap pertained to the Recent Site.

ASSOCIATED MATERIAL

Recent
Metal button, 34A-22/6 (Fig. 23d)
Metal box strap fragment, 34A-8h/13 (Fig. 24)

Pre-Columbian
2 chert rectangular/oval bifaces, 34A-23/7, 34A-25/9 (Fig. 27B:19d)
9 chert flakes, 34A/6, 8, 9, 11, 14
3 prismatic blade fragments of gray obsidian, 34A/8, 9
Used flake of gray obsidian, 34A-33/14
Quartzite mano fragment, reused as a hammerstone, 34A-31/11
Elongate soft stone object fragment, 34A-27/9
Fragment of a worked freshwater mussel, 34A-26/9
Fragment of an unidentifiable bone artifact, 34A-21/4
Fragment of an unworked bird longbone, 34A-32/14
Fragment of a centrally perforated sherd disk, 34A/10
Bar-shaped worked sherd, 34A-28/9 (Fig. 27B:138b)
2 Late Classic pottery figurine fragments, 34A-34a, b/14
2 pottery censer fragments, 34A/6, 7
Classic period sherds

TIME-SPAN 2

The occupation of RS 5F-1 (lots 1D/6, 34A/1, 2, 12).

In addition to the packed earth floor, features associated with the occupation of the structure included the hearth of three stones located at approximately the middle of the western wall and a large oblong patch of white plaster in the eastern part of the building. The hearth stones were charred and fire-cracked and the soil between them was dark gray and ashy in appearance.

The patch measured 3.25 by 1.05 m and was between 12 and 14 cm thick. A few chunks of rock between 5 and 6 cm in length had been incorporated into the lower portion of the patch. The upper surface was smooth. The patch began just inside the southern border, indicating it had been laid down after the foundation. Two box strap fragments, a pre-Columbian metate fragment, a small deposit of charcoal, and a hole 8 cm in diameter were found upon its rather soft surface (Fig. 15). At present the function of this plaster patch is unknown. The large surface area suggests it supported some kind of activity for which the dirt floor was considered unsuitable. Reina (pers. comm., 1964) felt that the patch could indicate a religious function for the structure. Mixed in with the plaster were 24 small weathered unidentifiable pre-Columbian sherds.

The surface and floor of the structure produced ca. 170 additional sherds. A water jar handle and two vessel body sherds from the on-floor lot, 34A/2, seemed to be the only ones contemporary with the occupation of the structure.

The in situ positions of pre-Columbian artifacts, such as the metate fragment, rubbing stone, and hammerstone, on the structure's floor indicate reuse by the inhabitants.

A kitchen was located at the western end of the building, where the hearth, two manos, parts of two large pottery bowls, and a water jar were found (Fig. 15). Most of the metal objects were recovered from the central and east-central areas of the floor (Fig. L35).

The cluster of materials outside the structure, collected as lot 1D/6, suggest domestic artifacts in temporary storage.

The material remains do not permit an estimate of the length of occupation of the structure. No signs of rebuilding or remodeling were noted. One can only observe that the orange grove surrounding the house indicates that the residents hoped to remain at least for the five years that it would take for the trees to bear fruit.

ASSOCIATED MATERIAL

Recent

Mano, 34A-4/2 (Fig. 18e)
Mano fragment, 34A-3/2 (Fig. 18f)
Metate, 1D-29/6 (Figs. 20, 21a)
Metate fragment, 34A-9/2 (Fig. 21b)
Fragment of an unclassified round object of ground stone, 34A-14/2
Fragment of the pelvis of a large bird, possibly turkey, 34A-15/2
Small unidentifiable fragment of flat bone from a small mammal, 34A/1
Small fragment of a wooden object that had a flat surface with a V-shaped groove, 34A-18/2 (Fig. 27B:156f)
Shotgun barrel, 34A-5/2 (Fig. 23a)
2 metal buttons, 34A-17/2, 34A-20/1 (Fig. 23d)
Fragments of at least two metal box straps, 34A-8/2, 34A-11/2 (Fig. 24)
2 machete fragments, 34A-6a/2, 34A-10/2 (Figs. 24, 25c)
Pottery pestle, 34A-7/2 (Fig. 25f)
Incomplete pottery jar, 34A-1/2 (Fig. 27c)
Large pottery bowl with everted rim, 34A-2/2 (Fig. 28c)
Incomplete large bowl with everted rim, 1D-31/6
Incomplete large pottery bowl with vertical lug handles, 1D-30/6
Bitter orange trees
Coconut palm

Pre-Columbian

2 chert flakes, burnt, 34A/2
Granite metate fragment, 34A-12/2
Rubbing stone fragment, 34A-12/2
Chert hammerstone, 34A-19/1
2 pottery censer fragments, 34A-1a, b/2

TIME-SPAN 1

The abandonment of RS 5F-1. It was hoped that the size of the trees growing within the stone foundation might indicate how long ago the building had been abandoned. But according to Lundell, the crucial trees were all of quick-growing species.

ADDITIONAL MATERIALS FOUND BY THE LAP

The following artifacts were recovered from floor surfaces exterior to the structure, especially to the north:

A large pre-Columbian chert biface "that was notched by the historic inhabitants to fasten it to a handle" (Palka 2005: fig. 6.29, upper left)
"Chert flakes, cutting tools, waste flakes, drills, and core fragments"
Metal projectile point (Palka 2005: fig. 7.26)
Metal box straps (Fig. L35)
Half of a pottery jar with a loop handle (Figs. L33, L43, L44)
Historic sherds

COMMENT

The excavation of the structure at RS 5F-1 demonstrated that it had been used as a dwelling and suggested it may have served non-residential functions as well. A domestic function is well documented by the hearth, the conventionally attributed uses of the associated items of material culture, and the grove of orange trees.

Non-residential functions are suggested by the location of the building close to at least three other Recent Sites, its large size and unique stone perimeter, and the interior oblong plaster patch. Reina pointed out the similarity of this patch to one in the church at San José. The San José example antedates the present church, but it is said by the inhabitants to mark the position of the altar in a former one. A bronze bell found at Tikal (Fig. 23f) is similar to, although smaller than, three bells now hanging in front of the San José church. Although the exact provenience of the Tikal bell is not known (Appendix F), it may have come from RS 5F-1.

A combination of domestic and religious functions in the same structure is unusual. Reina suggests that the western or domestic portion of the building might have been separated from the eastern or public part by a north-south partition. Another possibility is that the building was originally constructed as a church and then later used as a residence. Perhaps the building was the residence of the community leader (Joel Palka, pers. comm. 1999).

Recent Site 5F-2, Lot 1D/3
(Figs. 2h, 3, 17, L36)

Map location: 5F 268S 201E, collected February 1, 1957, by Vivian Broman and William R. Coe (Fig. 17). This locus was also investigated by the LAP, and was determined to be part of a two-house cluster excavated as Operations 5 and 6 (Table 2.3; Palka 2005:159–60, figs. 6.27, 6.28). Two hearths were recorded.

ASSOCIATED MATERIAL
Recent
Mano end fragment, 1D-7/3 (Fig. 18b)
Unclassified round limestone artifact, probably a pestle, 1D-27/3 (Fig. 21f)
Machete fragment, 1D-18/3 (Fig. 25b)
Incomplete indented-fillet bowl, red paint on exterior, 1D-16a/3 (Fig. 26f)
Nearly complete jar, 1D-22/3 (Fig. 27a), and the neck of another, 1D-15/3
Small pottery bowl, 1D-14/3 (Fig. 27f)
Incomplete large bowl with vertical lug handles, red paint or slip, 1D-17/3 (Fig. 28a)
4 incomplete large bowls with everted rims, 1D-16b, c/3, 1D-19/3, 1D-20/3
"[P]iece of china" left in the field
Bitter orange trees
Mexican hat palms (*Chamaedorea cataractarum*)

Possibly pre-Columbian
A complete and an incomplete mortar of dolomite, the local bedrock, 1D-26a, b/3 (Fig. 27B:91c)

ADDITIONAL MATERIALS FOUND BY THE LAP
Limestone grinding stone fragment
Animal bones, including deer and peccary
Glass medicine bottle with "Barry's Tricopherous for the Skin and Hair, New York" in raised letters (Palka 2005: fig. 7.23d)
Metal hoop earring (Palka 2005: fig. 7.27)
A long thick metal needle
"[W]orked pieces of machetes, one of which may have been used as a spear point" (possibly shown in Palka 2005: fig. 7.25, lower right)
Historic potsherds

From the middens to the south and east of this residence the LAP recovered the following (Palka 2005:160):

"Chert tools and flakes"
Unidentified metal fragments
A trigger mechanism and two firing hammers from muzzle-loading shotguns (Palka 2005: fig. 7.24f)
Metal gunpowder flask (Palka 2005: fig. 7.24a)
Piece of round shot
White earthenware fragments

COMMENT

The presence and distribution of surface materials, bitter orange trees, four to six Mexican hat palms, and a hearth of three stones indicated a house belonging to the Tikal aldea. Subsequent excavation by the LAP suggests there were actually two residences at this site.

Recent Site 5F-3, Lot 1D/7
(Figs. 2h, 3, L37, L38)

Map location: 5F 276S 35E. Collected on May 2, 1957 by Vivian Broman, James E. Hazard, and Edwin M. Shook. Excavated as Operations 2 and 3 by the LAP in 1998 (Table 2.3; Palka 2005:156–58, fig. 6.23-6.25).

In her field notes Broman (1957:41) mentions a group of five stones, perhaps representing metates or a hearth. Other materials were found in two groups, ca. 7.5 m apart, suggesting the former presence of two houses. A cocoyol palm (*Acrocomia mexicana*) was associated with RS 5F-3. Excavations by the LAP established the presence of two hearths.

ASSOCIATED MATERIAL
Recent
Incomplete pottery pestle, 1D-11/7 (Fig. 25g)
Incomplete indented-fillet bowl, 1D-32/7 (Fig. 26g)
Burned fragment of a jar, 1D-33/7
2 incomplete large bowls with everted rims, 1D-34/7, 1D-35/7
Cocoyol palm

ADDITIONAL MATERIALS FOUND BY THE LAP
Small chert biface (Palka 2005: fig. 7.16 center)
Chert scraper (Palka 2005: fig. 7.16 right)

Chert bifacial "pounder" (Palka 2005: fig. 7.16 left)
Chert blades
Chert flakes
Animal bones, unidentified, in small fragments
Iron or steel axe head
Metal artifact fragments, unidentified
Painted imported white earthenware vessels (Fig. L37; Palka 2005: figs. 7.23a, 7.28)
"[M]any Historic ceramics" including large jars, a flaring-walled serving vessel (Fig. L45), large round cooking vessel, and small round-lipped hemispherical bowls (Palka 2005: figs. 7.5, 7.6)
Charcoal

Some of the artifacts listed above came from a sheet midden about 10 m to the east of Operation 3, perhaps a dumping place for several households (Palka 2005:157–58). The midden also included fragments of glass bottles.

COMMENT

The distribution of the artifacts suggests two houses at this site, both well provisioned with durable goods.

Recent Site 5F-4, Lot 1D/8
(Figs. 2h, 3)

Map location: 5F 245S 126E. This site was noted by Vivian Broman and Edwin M. Shook on May 2, 1957, but nothing was collected from it.

Broman (1957:41) mentions a hearth of three stones with a metate near them.

COMMENT

The location suggests that RS 5F-4 was a house pertaining to the Tikal aldea.

Recent Site 5F-5, Lot 1D/5
(Figs. 2h, 3)

Map location: 5F 405S 124E according to the lot card made out by Broman in 1957, but incorrectly located on the Tikal Map (TR. 11) at 5F 280S 68E. This site was collected on May 11, 1957, by James E. Hazard and Vivian Broman.

A concentration of pottery was exposed by a fallen tree and was found buried in humus to a depth of ca. 30 cm. The collection included fragments of one, or possibly two, pre-Columbian flanged chimney censers and an unknown number of sherds that I could not locate for examination.

COMMENT

No Historic material could be identified with certainty from this site. Therefore it is no longer considered a Recent Site.

Recent Site 7E-1, Lot 1D/12 (Fig. 2i)

Map location: ca. 7E 360S 480E. William Haviland (pers. comm. 2007) brought to my attention the fact that a metal corn mill and rusty machete blade found in 1961 by workmen to the north of the Tikal-Remate Road and east of the Corriental Aguada were associated with a lime tree. The presence of the lime tree suggests this locus may have been part of the late 19th century Tikal aldea. It is not indicated as a Recent Site on the Tikal map.

ASSOCIATED MATERIAL
Recent
Iron corn mill and handle, 1D-78a, b/12 (Fig. 22m)
Steel or iron machete blade, of the Collins (smooth) type, about 12 inches (ca. 30 cm) long and very rusted. It was not catalogued and could not be located in 1964.
Lime tree

Recent Materials Collected as Single Finds or of Lost Provenience

Whole mano, 1C-37/9 (Fig. 18a), discovered in front of Str. 5D-48 of Gp. 5D-11 near RS 5D-2

Whole mano with reshaped end, 1C-46/9 (Fig. 18c), without provenience
Whole mano, 2B-20/3 (Fig. 18d), from the vicinity of the Tikal Aguada (Fig. 2g)
Whole mano, uncatalogued (Fig. 18g), from Gp. 5D-2, shaped from a fragment of St. 6
Large flat metate, 1N-1/1 (Fig. 21c), from the vicinity of Strs. 3E-41 and 3E-42 (Fig. 2b), shaped from a carved altar
3 beer bottles from Str. 5C-17, the stela enclosure of St. 16 and Alt. 5, of Gp. 5C-1 (Fig. 2d), 1C-32/8 (Fig. 22f; Appendix J), 43C-65/2 (Fig. 22j), and 43C-66/16 (Fig. 22k)
Whole glass bottle, 1C-51/1 (Fig. 22a), without provenience
Iron cooking pot handle fragment identical to the handles on the pot shown in Fig. 22l, from the Great Plaza of Gp. 5D-2, 11H-3/3
3 shot from the vicinity of the Tikal Aguada and the Tikal Airfield, 2B-6/1, 2B-7/1, and the North Terrace of Gp. 5D-2, 12B-49/9 (all Fig. 23b)
Bronze bell without clapper, 1D-12/4 (Fig. 23f), without provenience, but possibly from RS 5F-1
Bayonet discovered near the southern terminus of the Tikal-Uaxactun Trail at ca. 4F 280S 20E. Kept as a souvenir by the finder (Appendix F)
Large knife, 117C-6/3 (Fig. 25d), found on Str. 5D-73 in Gp. 5D-2
Pottery pipe stem fragment, 4J-2/1 (Fig. 25e), from a roofcomb chamber of Str. 5D-1, Temple I, in Gp. 5D-2
Mamey tree or trees (*Pouteria sapota*) in the general area of RS 5F-1 through 5F-4
At least one sweet orange tree (*Citrus sinensis*) in the vicinity of the Tikal Aguada

Material Culture

General Considerations

SUMMARY OF RECENT MATERIAL CULTURE

In the figure references 27B is TR. 27, Part B, 33A is TR. 33, Part A, 37 is TR. 37, and L is Appendix L on the CD-ROM that accompanies this volume.

Number	Type	Figure	Page
7	Manos, ground stone	33A:10c, 37:18a-g	81
6	Metates, ground stone	33A:65k, l, 37:18h, 19, 20, 21a-c, e	81–84
3	Miscellaneous ground stone	37:21d, f	84
11	Bottles, glass	37:22a-k	85
3	Buttons, metal	37:23d	86
3	Shot, metal	37:23b	86
3	Machete fragments, metal	37:24, 25b, c	87, 88
2	Miscellaneous worked fragments, metal	37:23e	86
1	Knife, metal	37:25d	88
1	Shotgun barrel, metal	37:23a	86
1	Cooking pot, metal	37:22 l	85
1	Cooking pot handle, metal		
2	Box straps in fragments, metal	37:24	87
1	Bell, metal	37:23f	86
1	Axe head, metal	37:23g	86
1	Pillbox, metal	37:23c	86
1	Chisel, metal	37:25a	88
1	Hand mill	37:22m	85
1	Bayonet, metal		
2	Pestles, pottery	37:25f, g	88
1	Pipe stem fragment, pottery	37:23e	86
1	Figurine fragment, pottery	37:26a	89
23	Large bowls with everted rims, pottery	37:28c-f	91
3	Large bowls with solid vertical lug handles, pottery	37:28a, b	91
1	Jar with strap handles, pottery	37:26c	89
9	Jars with loop handles, pottery	37:27a-d	90
3	Pitchers, pottery	37:26d, e	89
2	Baking dish rim fragments, pottery	37:26b	89
3	Bowls with rounded and flaring sides, pottery	37:27e-g	90
3	Small ringstand bowls, pottery	37:28g-i	91
3	Bowls with indented fillet, pottery	37:26f-h	89
1	Unclassified worked fragment, wood	27B:156f	
2	Unworked fragments, bone		
	Exotic plants		

Surviving Recent Site material culture was a mix of imported, machine-made manufactured goods of metal and glass, handmade goods of ground stone and pottery that were of local or regional origin, and salvaged pre-Columbian stone artifacts. Stylistic resemblances to pottery from Yucatán (Fig. 29; Thompson 1958) and San José (Fig. 14; Reina and Hill 1978) suggest that most of the vessels found at Tikal had been brought there. This is certainly the case for the sherds of decorated white earthenware recovered by the LAP (Fig. L37; Palka 2005: figs. 7.23a, 7.28). On the other hand, the polishing stones and worked sherd recovered from RS 4F-5 strongly suggest that pottery production was also carried out locally. Unworked materials were rare. Bone succumbed to the poor conditions for its preservation and only two pieces were recovered. No shells of the freshwater snails *Pomacea flagellata* and *Pachychilus* spp., still occasionally eaten in the area today, were associated with any of the Recent Sites. The exotic fruit trees and palms that were still present in the 1960s are additional evidence for subsistence. We can assume that a diverse assemblage of locally produced baskets, mats, furniture, and other household items, as well as store-bought clothing or at least cloth, was also once present.

The 19th-century settlers made frequent use of easily scavenged pre-Columbian flaked and ground stone artifacts that are so plentiful at Tikal, such as chert bifaces, scrapers, scraper-awls, and flakes, and ground stone manos, metate fragments, celts, and pieces of carved and plain stone monuments. These pre-Columbian artifacts are described and illustrated in TR. 27B. On the other hand, nodules of chert are still easy to find at Tikal, so it is possible that some of the flakes associated with Recent Sites represent expedient cutting and scraping tools made by the settlers. But at present I don't know how they could be distinguished from pre-Columbian examples.

Descriptions

Artifacts of Ground Stone

For their manos and metates and other ground stone artifacts, the settlers made use of the readily accessible soft, bedded, light-colored limestone of the Late Classic period monuments. This is seen most dramatically in a metate (Figs. 37:20, 21a), which was made from a fragment of St. 21 (TR. 33A: figs. 31, 97b). Only one mano (Fig. 37:18g) and one metate (Fig. 37:21c) were made of the harder limestone used for Early Classic monuments. In addition to their form, marks made by metal tools also distinguish Recent ground stone artifacts from earlier ones.

Variety A cigar-shaped manos and Variety A tripod-slab metates like those found at Tikal were widely used in Mesoamerica until metal hand mills (Fig. 37:22m) became available, and they are still in use in remote areas (e.g., Cook 1982; Nelson 1987).

MANOS

Figure 37:18c-g

Total: seven examples, five of which are complete. Manos were classified into two varieties based on overall form.

Variety A manos were long and well formed with round cross sections (Fig. 37:18a, b, d, f). There were five, three of which were complete.

Variety B manos were long with irregular quadrilateral cross sections. Only one face was used for grinding (Fig. 37:18c, e). There were two examples, both complete.

The lengths of the complete manos ranged between 17.4 and 36.0 cm, and weights ranged between ca. 4 lb 3 oz (ca. 1909 gm) and ca. 5 lb 7 oz (ca. 2479 gm).

Manos were found at RS 5F-1, 5F-2, and on the surface in front of Str. 5D-48 of Gp. 5D-11, Gp. 5D-2, and near the Tikal Aguada. The provenience of one is unknown.

METATES

Figures 37:18h, 19, 20, 21a-c, e

Total: six, five of which are complete. Metates were classified into two varieties based upon the presence or absence of supports.

Variety A was a well-made thick slab on three low supports (Figs. 37:18, 20, 21a). There were two examples, both complete.

Variety B was a thick slab without supports. There were four examples, three of which were complete (Figs. 33A:65k, l; 37:19,21b, c, e).

Lengths of the complete metates ranged from 35 to 43 cm, widths from 26.1 to 33.0 cm, and heights from 9.5 to 17.0 cm.

Metates were found in RS 2G-1, 4F-3, 5F-1, and in the North Zone near Str. 3E-48.

MISCELLANEOUS GROUND STONE ARTIFACTS

Fig. 37:21d, f

Total: three, one complete.

This group of artifacts of uncertain function and use consists of two spherical objects that may be pecking stones or pestles (Fig. 37:21f), of which one is complete, and the end of a large, charred cigar-shaped object too large to have been a mano (Fig. 37:21d). All were shaped with metal tools.

The large cigar-shaped fragment was found in RS 4F-3. The spherical objects came from RS 5F-1 and 5F-2.

Artifacts of Glass

Bottles were the only objects of glass recovered. Three can be associated with the Tikal aldea, while the others appear to be later.

BOTTLES

Figure 37:22a-k

Total: 11, 10 whole, 1 broken but essentially complete. Six varieties were defined.

Variety A originally probably held wine. There was one example of dark green glass with a concave base (Fig. 37:22e). It was blown, rather than pressed, and had a cork stopper. It is 24.7 cm tall.

Variety B bottles were probably used for medicine. There is one example of pale green glass with a concave base. It had a cork stopper and was probably blown (Fig. 37:22b). It is 23.5 cm tall.

Variety C is a gin bottle. There was one deep olive green example with the slight iridescence acquired by buried glass. It has a square cross section, concave base, and was probably blown, and had a cork stopper (Fig. 37:22a). This form is old, going back to the 17th century (e.g., Cotter 1958: pl. 84). These bottles were used to ship gin and were squared for more efficient packing. Our example is 22.8 cm tall.

Variety D consists of beer bottles. There are four examples of pressed, pale greenish glass with crown caps. All bear the names of their New York breweries: Welz & Zerweck (Fig. 37:22f), further described by Paul S. Newton in Appendix J, Rubsum and Horrmann (Fig. 37:22j), and F & M Schaeffer (Fig. 37:22k). Heights are 23.0, 23.4, 24.5 cm, respectively.

Variety E are small bottles, all of pressed, pale green glass with cork stoppers. One is marked with the name of John H. Williams & Co., of New York and the name of the product it originally contained, Agua de la Reina (Fig. 37:22c), further described by Paul S. Newton in Appendix J. According to Newton's research, this bottle would have to be older than 1860, which was the year the Williams Company went out of business. The other two examples are plain (Fig. 37:22d, h).

Heights are 23.6, 22.5, 23.7 cm, respectively.

Variety F is a small bottle graduated in ounces, with a capacity of 6 oz. There was one example made of colorless pressed glass with a cork stopper (Fig. 37:22i). It was 16.6 cm tall.

Bottles were found in RS 2G-1, 4B-1, 4F-2, and 4F-4. Three beer bottles came from Str. 5C-17, the enclosure of St. 16 of Twin Pyramid Group 5C-1, and were most likely discarded by members of the Hays-Cruz Boundary Commission in 1930 (Appendix E; TR. 27A: Appendix 8). One beer bottle and the intriguing Variety C gin bottle are without provenience.

Artifacts of Metal

There are several types of metal artifacts, most of them associated with the Tikal aldea. The house at RS 5F-1 proved to be especially rich. Many examples are parts of composite tools made of durable and perishable materials. Like their pre-Columbian chert and obsidian counterparts, their handles and fastenings of wood or horn have completely vanished.

BUTTONS

Figure 37:23d

Total: three complete. Two varieties were defined.

Variety A was sewn on. There is one example of brass and one of iron or steel. Each has four holes and a diameter of 1.7 cm.

Variety B was wired onto its backing. It is of iron or steel with a border that appears to be made of brass. It has a diameter of 2.0 cm.

All examples were found at RS 5F-1.

SHOT

Figure 37:23b

Total: three complete. Two are of lead with a maximum diameter of 1.6 cm and one is of iron with a maximum diameter of 2.25 cm.

The iron shot and one of the lead balls were found during the construction of the Tikal airfield. The other lead shot comes from the surface of the North Terrace of Gp. 5D-2.

MACHETES

Figures 37:24, 25b, c

Total: three incomplete. All were made of steel. Two

varieties are represented.

Variety A, or Collins type of machete, has a smooth blade (Fig. 37:25b). The original Collins machete was manufactured by the Collins Axe Factory in Collinsville, Connecticut, from 1845 until the factory closed in 1966. However, the name is often applied to all machetes with smooth blades, regardless of actual brand (<www.wikipedia.org/wiki/machete, http://en.wikipedia.org/wiki/Collinsville, Connecticut>, accessed March 2009). There were two incomplete examples of this type, one of which was lost.

Variety B, referred to by Peteneros as a "lagarto" machete, has three parallel, lengthwise grooves on each side of the blade (Figs. 37:16, 17c; Palka 2005: fig. 7.18i). It was made in England and was traded into the Petén from British Honduras. It was later supplanted by the Collins type of machete from the United States (Antonio Ortiz, pers. comm. 1963). There was one example that consists of a squared tip fragment beveled on one face.

One Collins type fragment was found at RS 5F-2 (Fig. 37:17b), the other at RS 7E-1. The lagarto fragment was found at RS 5F-1.

KNIFE
Figure 37:25d

Total: one.

It was found on Str. 5D-73 of Gp. 5D-2, which borders the Great Plaza.

SHOTGUN BARREL
Figure 37:23a

Total: one. The corroded, but complete barrel of a single-barrel, front-loading, closed cylinder shotgun came from RS 5F-1. No trade name was visible. Maximum length is 64.0 cm. The inner diameter of the muzzle is 1.0 cm.

TRIPOD COOKING POTS
Figure 37:22l

Total: one example, badly corroded but nearly complete, and a handle fragment from another pot of the same type.

The nearly complete pot has two vertical, angled handles and three short, pointed feet. Its total height is 15.7 cm. The handle fragment is 2.4 cm long.

The cooking pot comes from RS 4F-5. The handle fragment came to light during excavations in the Great Plaza of Gp. 5D-2.

BOX STRAPS
Figure 37:24

Total: two straps in several fragments. These thin iron or steel straps were said by the workmen to have been used to bind boxes. The straps are perforated and hooks and nails were still attached to them. One is 2.4 cm wide, the other 2.7 cm wide. Both came from the floor of the house at RS 5F-1.

BELL
Figure 37:23f

Total: one, well preserved, missing the handle and clapper. This bell, of cast bronze, was decorated with an obscured design in low relief. The lower border of the bell is in good condition, suggesting that it was not sounded by beating the edge, as is the case with the bronze bells that hung outside the church in the village of San José Petén. Greatest diameter: 12.8 cm.

According to E.M. Shook (Appendix F), the bell was found around 1950 by Rafael Caseres, one of the Government workers constructing the airfield. Although the bell was catalogued as from RS 4F-4, lot 1D/4, this provenience is probably incorrect. Caseres told Shook that he had found the bell southeast of the Tikal Aguada. Shook felt that the bell could have come from the cluster of RS 5F-1 through 5F-4.

AXE HEAD
Figure 37:23g

Total: one, corroded but complete. This large axe head, of iron or steel, had an oblong perforation for a now-vanished wooden shaft. No trade name was visible. Greatest length: 17.8 cm. It was found at RS 2G-1.

PILLBOX
Figure 37:23c

Total: one, complete. It is of iron or steel and so corroded that it could no longer be opened. It has a round plan and a diameter of 4.1 cm. It was found at RS 2G-1.

CHISEL

Figure 37:25a

Total: one, corroded but complete, made or iron or steel. The wooden handle has completely vanished. Greatest length: 34.0 cm. It came from RS 5D-2.

HAND MILL

Figure 37:22m

Total: one, nearly complete, missing the wooden grip for the handle and the screw connecting the handle to the mill. Presumably made of iron or steel. Height excluding the attachment screw is 31.3.cm.

The mill, "La Campana," was made by the C.S. Bell Company of Hillsboro, Ohio, U.S.A. Traces of color on the attachment screw indicate that the mill was once affixed to a surface painted with glossy red enamel. Hand mills of this kind are used by small communities throughout the Petén and have generally supplanted stone manos and metates. The families of the workmen excavating at Tikal in the 1960s ordered similar mills from Guatemala City.

The mill was found in RS 7E-1, lying on the ground near a lime tree and in association with a corroded Variety A machete blade of the Collins type.

MISCELLANEOUS FLAT STEEL FRAGMENTS

Figure 37:23e

Total: two reworked machete fragments, probably used as tools of some kind (cf. Clark 1991a, 1991b).

The fragments were found lying near each other on the floor of the house at RS 5F-1.

BAYONET

Total: one, apparently complete. E.M. Shook (Appendix F) reported that in 1957 a bayonet was discovered near the trail from Tikal to Uaxactun, at approximately 4F 20E 280S. Its finder, Colonel Ramiro Gereda Asturias of the Guatemalan Army, thought that it belonged to a 19th-century weapon. He kept the bayonet as a souvenir.

Artifacts of Modeled Pottery

PESTLES

Figure 37:25f, g

Total: two, one complete. The whole example has a small, pinched, nose-like protuberance on one side of the handle (Fig. 37:17f). It was identified as a pestle by the workmen who found it.

The complete pestle was found at RS 5F-1 and the fragment is from RS 5F-3.

PIPE

Figure 37:25e

Total: one small stem fragment of white pottery only 3.4 cm long, with an outer diameter of 0.6 cm and a central perforation of 0.15 cm. Antonio Ortiz observed that it is of a type used by chicleros around the turn of the century.

It was found in Gp. 5D-2, in one of the chambers of the roof comb of Str. 5D-1, Great Temple I.

Pottery Vessels

The pottery vessels found at Tikal Recent Sites shared the following characteristics: simple shape, almost complete absence of decoration, relatively massive walls and bases, and coarse calcite temper. They were readily distinguishable from pre-Columbian pots and sherds. Most were identical to vessel types produced from at least the 1940s through 1960s in San José Petén (Figs. 14, L33, L43, L44; Palka 2005: fig. 7.10; Reina and Hill 1978: fig. 41). Most of the vessel surfaces were unslipped and undecorated. However, a group of three bowls were exceptional. All were embellished with indented fillets. One had a dull red exterior slip (Fig. 37:26f) and two others had unique notched rims (Fig. 37:26g, h). These traits were not observed at San José, but do occur, for example, in Yucatán (Fig. 29; Thompson 1958:58, 63, figs. 11f, 12d, f, j, 13a-c, e, 35c, f-h, 36d, l).

Rubén Reina studied pottery making at San José and purchased a collection of 11 vessels and 1 candlestick, which served as our reference collection. The shapes and ware of pottery vessels recovered from the Tikal aldea (Figs. 26–28) matched those in the reference collection, as well as vessels recorded from San José around 1940 (Fig. 14; Reina and Hill 1978: fig. 41). Interestingly, a comparison of the vertical lug handles of Figure 28a and b with Figure 14b suggests that 14b was incorrectly drawn.

The pottery vessels found with the Tikal aldea appear to have at least three sources. The close resemblance between the San José and several of the Tikal pottery vessels brings up the likelihood that most of the pottery vessels used in the aldea came from San José. On the other hand, the four jadeite celts, chert polishing stone, and worked sherd found at RS 4F-5 indicate at least some local production. The indented-fillet bowls, low ringstands, and red paint suggest contact with Yucatán (Thompson 1958:58, 63). Instrument paste analyses of the Tikal and San José pottery vessels and sherds could most likely determine where the vessels found at Tikal were made. Visual inspection at high magnification might also be informative. For example, T. Patrick Culbert, who is reporting on the pre-Columbian ceramics of Tikal, has determined that Early Postclassic Caban Complex pottery found at Tikal was most likely produced around Lake Petén Itzá. Its non-local origin is indicated by tiny shells in the paste (T. Patrick Culbert, pers. comm. 2009).

The close resemblance of Recent Tikal pottery to that of mid-20th-century San José Petén is a good indicator of the regional affiliation and residential nature of the Tikal aldea, even though it does not provide much information on chronology.

If we accept the accounts of the Yucatecan origins of the aldea settlers, the recovered material culture indicates that they established economic, as well as administrative, ties with San José Petén when the aldea came under San José's jurisdiction. San José seems to have provided the aldea with at least some of its pottery vessels, and probably other perishable and durable goods, as well.

The following classification of eight types is based upon vessel form.

LARGE BOWLS WITH EVERTED RIM AND ROUND BASE

Figures 37:14a, 28c-f, L27

Total: 23, 1 whole, 20 restorable or reconstructible. These correspond to San José *ollas* (Reina and Hill 1978: fig. 41a). All of the examples from Tikal, as well as 2 from our San José reference collection, show heavy burning from use as cooking pots. Maudslay pictures 2 such bowls [1889–1902: pl. 80(b)]. A similar form is identified as a cooking pot by Thompson (1958: figs. 12a, 34e).

Range of height: 12.2 to 26.0 cm, range of greatest diameter (many have oval orifices): 19.0 to 37.6 cm

This form was identified at RS 2G-1, 4B-1, 4F-2, 4F-3, 4F-4, 5F-1, 5F-2, and 5F-3.

LARGE BOWLS WITH INCURVED RIM AND VERTICAL LUG HANDLES

Figures 37: 14b, 28a, b, L26

Total: three, reconstructible. These correspond to San José *tamaleros* (Reina and Hill 1978: fig. 41b). The example in the San José reference collection is heavily smudged inside and out. This is not the case with the Tikal examples, and perhaps they were used for storage or serving. The exterior of one bowl (Fig. 37:28a) was painted dull red.

Range of height: 14.0, over 17.0, and over 22.0 cm

Greatest diameters, excluding handles: 30.0, ca. 23.0, and 32.0 cm

This form occurred at RS 4F-3, 5F-1, and 5F-2.

JAR WITH STRAP HANDLES

Figure 37:26c

Total: one, reworked.

The neck of this small jar had been cut away and it was reused as a cooking pot, as demonstrated by heavy smudging.

Height: 11.5 cm

Diameter: 18.8 cm

It was found in RS 5D-1, together with a whole pitcher (Fig. 37:26d).

JARS WITH LOOP HANDLES

Figures 37:14f, 27a-d

Total: nine, five reconstructible.

The shape of this vessel type indicates it was used for water and other liquids. They are referred to as *cánteros* in San José (Reina and Hill 1978: fig. 41f). None of the jars from Tikal or in the San José reference collection showed burning or smudging.

Range of height: 19.8–34.4 cm

Range of diameter excluding handles: 17.4–35.2 cm

Jars with loop handles were found at RS 2G-1, 4F-1, 4F-2, 4F-3, 5D-1, 5F-1, 5F-2, and 5F-3.

PITCHERS

Figures 37:14e, 26d, e

Total: three, one whole, one almost complete.

Pitchers are known as *batidores* in San José (Reina and Hill 1978: fig. 41e). The Tikal examples, although not the one in the San José collection, show some exterior blackening. They were probably used for cooking, as well as for serving. A heavily burned base fragment from RS 4F-5 may have been used as a small griddle.

Range of height: 12.8–14.7 cm

Range of greatest diameter excluding handle: 12.2, 14.0, and 15.3 cm

Pitchers were recovered from RS 4F-4, 4F-5, and 5D-1.

SHALLOW PLATTER OR LID

Figures 37:14c, 26b, L26

Total: one. Two non-fitting rim sherds seem to pertain to the same platter or lid. Both fragments show burning.

The San José pottery reference collection included a baking dish cover or *tapadera* (Reina and Hill 1978: fig. 41c) and platter that suggests the Tikal sherds came from a similar baking dish set. The San José set consists of a lid 42.5 cm in diameter and a bowl of 42 cm diameter. The bowl is much darker in color than the lid, which is explained by the mode of use of the set. Similar forms were also produced in Yucatán (Thompson 1958: fig. 34). In the Petén, this type of baking set is used to bake food such as *arepa,* a small cake made of cornmeal, sugar, lard, and cinnamon. The cover is preheated and then placed over the bowl, which rests in a bed of hot coals (Aura Luz de Ortiz, pers. comm. 1964; cf. Redfield and Villa Rojas 1934:231).

Rim thickness: 0.9 cm

Both sherds were found in RS 4F-2.

SMALL BOWLS WITH ROUNDED OR FLARING SIDES

Figure 37:27e-g

Total: three, two restorable.

In regions where they have not been replaced by enamelware (Figs. L27, L28) or china, such small plain bowls are primarily used for individual servings of everyday food (Thompson 1958:107). Where enamel or china is used for everyday eating, pottery bowls of this type are restricted to ceremonial use (Fig. L28; Redfield and Villa Rojas 1934:36; Reina 1962:30, 33; Villa Rojas 1945:33). However, the fragment of the largest bowl was burned suggesting larger examples were used as cooking vessels.

Height: 6.3, 11.0, and ca. 13.0 cm

Greatest diameter: 16.5, 22.0 cm

Small rounded-base bowls came from RS 2G-1, 4F-2, and 5F-2.

SMALL BOWLS WITH LOW RINGSTANDS

Figure 37:28g-i

Total: three, two reconstructible.

Vessels of this type were not included in the San José collection. Their size suggests dinnerware. However, the pedestal base, which does not occur at San José, seems closer to Yucatán, where larger pedestal-base bowls are used as water coolers or incense burners (Redfield and Villa Rojas 1934: pl. 5b; Thompson 1958: figs. 14, 32, 42).

Height: 5.8, 8.0 cm

Greatest diameter: ca. 13.5, 12.1 cm

Two came from RS 4F-2 and one from 4F-5.

BOWLS WITH FLAT BASE, INCURVING RIM, AND INDENTED FILLET FIGURE 37:18F-H

Total: three, one whole.

The bowl from RS 5F-2 (Fig. 37:14f) differs from the others in having a dull red exterior, a rim without indentations, and a fillet formed by appliqué rather than pinching. None of these bowls showed burning.

Reina's study collection from San José had no vessels with indented-fillet decoration and I was not able to find exact counterparts of the Tikal examples in the literature. On the other hand, Thompson (1958: figs. 35f, g, h, 36c, d, l) illustrates bowls with plain fillets from Yucatán that are similar in shape. The Yucatán bowls are described as cooking pots or water basins. Indented fillets were used as design elements on pre-Columbian Lowland Maya pottery vessels as early as the Late Preclassic period (Laura Kosakowsky, pers. comm. 2008).

Height: 12.0, 13.4 cm

Greatest diameter excluding fillet: 24.9, 28.0, 29.0 cm

Bowls with indented fillets were found at RS 2G-1, 5F-2, and 5F-3.

Exotic Plants

In addition to the indigenous trees with edible fruit found at Tikal (Figs. L29, L30) the residents of the Tikal aldea also planted exotic species (Figs. L31, L32). These may also be considered material culture. The principal sources for information presented here are conversations with C.L. Lundell (pers. comm. 1962–1964) and his invaluable monograph on the vegetation of the Petén (Lundell 1937). Dennis Puleston was able to locate other exotic trees (Appendix G).

SPECIES: *Citrus aurantium* (Bitter, or Seville Orange), *Citrus aurantifolia* (Lime), *Citrus sinensis* (Sweet Orange)

Citrus trees do not grow wild in the Petén so their presence indicates they were intentionally planted. In the Tikal area, bitter orange trees begin to bear fruit when they are about five years old. Where they are kept free of native vegetation and have sufficient light, they take on a bushy appearance and bear fruit (Fig. L31). However, they get crowded out in the forest. The trees grow very tall and spindly in their efforts to reach the light, do not bear fruit, and are difficult to identify as exotics. It is more than likely that some citrus trees were misidentified or overlooked altogether.

Several bitter orange trees and at least three lime trees were associated with RS 4F-2, 4F-3, 4F-4, 4F-5, 5F-1, 5F-2, and 7E-1. Maler noted that there were orange and lime trees between the Tikal Aguada and the camping place of his men in Gp. 5E-11 (Fig. 2f, g), probably the trees associated with the abandoned aldea. In the 1960s and early 1970s there was at least one, much appreciated sweet orange tree near the Tikal Aguada that still bore fruit.

SPECIES: *Sabal mexicana* Mart. (Mexican hat palm)

Between four and six trees were associated with RS 5F-2. In his description of RS 5F-2, Edwin M. Shook (pers. comm. 1962) mentioned two palms and several orange trees. In 1963 Antonio Ortiz and I located one palm in the extremely dense secondary vegetation, but we found no orange trees in its immediate vicinity. In 1964 another excursion to Map Square 5F with C.L. Lundell located four Mexican hat palms and two dead orange trees. Three of the palm trees had been planted about 9 m apart in a straight line running approximately east to west, while the fourth palm was about

9 m to the southwest of the second tree in the row of three. The presence of the orange trees suggested that the locale was RS 5F-2.

Lundell has never encountered the Mexican hat palm growing wild on the Yucatán peninsula (1937:53). It is often planted in the villages of the northern Petén. The young leaves are used to make hats.

SPECIES: *Acrocomia mexicana* (cocoyol palm)

During the summer of 1963 workmen identified a cocoyol palm, said to be a native of the savanna country to the south. The palm was approximately 30 m north of Str. 5F-27, in the vicinity of RS 5F-3.

In 1964 Lundell confirmed the identification as cocoyol. Its usual habitat is grasslands and marginal forest. This palm was evidently planted at Tikal for its edible nuts and fruits. In Yucatán, cocoyol nuts are strung together with animal bones and hooves and small snail and oyster shells to make amulets for children to protect them from illness (Redfield and Villa Rojas 1934:176–77, pl. 15a).

SPECIES: *Calocarpum mammosum* (mamey)

Lundell found one mamey tree in Square 5F in the vicinity of RS 5F-1 through 5F-4. It was known to the workmen, who occasionally gathered the fruit.

Mameys are large trees and require deep soil. They are rare in the northern Petén. The tree at Tikal could well have been intentionally planted, perhaps by the 19th-century settlers.

SPECIES: *Cocos nucifera* (coconut palm)

During the summer of 1963, Dennis Puleston discovered a small coconut palm in the vicinity of RS 5F-1 (Appendix G). Reina observed coconut palms at San José in the late 1950s (Rubén Reina, pers. comm. 1961, see Appendix H).

Appendix E
Published Records of Visits to Tikal, 1696–1956

1696

Father Andrés de Avendaño, fleeing from Lake Petén Itzá to Yucatán, may have been the first European to see Tikal. This was a year before the subjugation of Tayasal by Martín de Ursua (Avendaño 1987:61–62; Jones 1998:219; Morley 1938:55).

1698

During the time of upheaval following the conquest of the Itza of Tayasal, a hamlet by the name of Tikal is mentioned as a place of refuge for the native population. It was said to be located about two days by road directly northeast of the settlement of Ketz on Lake Petén Itzá (Jones 1998:350).

1848

Ambrosio Tut, also written as Ambrocio Tut, Governor of the Petén, and Colonel Modesto Méndez, Corregidor of the Petén (Fig. L15), spent six days exploring Tikal (Hammond 1987; Méndez 1955; Morley 1938:206). Tut and Méndez had, of course, received prior word of the ruins. The credit for the actual sighting of Tikal may belong to a group of hunters from the Indian village of Chúntukel, about 65 km west-northwest of Tikal (Maler 1910:150; Morley 1938:76–77).

1852

Modesto Méndez's second visit to Tikal (Hammond 1987).

1869, 1890

Capt. John Carmichael of the British Army, based in British Honduras, made two visits to Tikal (Cerezo 1951:8). Cerezo says that Carmichael brought back to Britain a story of treasure at Tikal that inspired the visits of Gann and Jolly, Herron, and Robson 40 years later.

1877

Dr. Carl Gustav Bernoulli (Fig. L16), an expatriate Swiss physician who had a finca in Retalhuleu, reached Tikal. He was accompanied by a young German botanist, O.R. Cario. Bernoulli's visit is of special interest. With the permission of the government of Guatemala, he arranged for the removal and transportation to Basle, Switzerland, of Lintel 3 of Temple IV, and he is the first explorer to mention the Tikal aldea (Maler 1911:42; Meyer-Holdampf 1997:101–11).

1879

Salvador Valenzuela, Inspector of Agriculture of the Guatemalan Government, spent four days at Tikal among the settlers (Appendix K; Valenzuela 1951).

Guatemalan soldiers were sent to Tikal "against the Indians" (Walter M. Wolfe 1901g; Appendix I).

1881, 1882

Two visits by the English explorer Alfred Percival Maudslay (Maudslay 1889–1902; Fig. L18).

1892

Federico Artes, who was specially commissioned by the Guatemalan Government, was to make molds and casts for display at the Columbian Exposition of 1893. According to Morley (1938:80), Artes found nothing of interest.

1895

The first of two visits by the Austrian explorer

Teobert Maler (Fig. L17), on behalf of the Peabody Museum of Archaeology and Ethnology at Harvard University (Maler 1908, 1911).

1901

Visit by Professor Walter M. Wolfe of Brigham Young University, Utah (Wolfe 1901a-g; Appendix I; Fig. L24).

1904

Teobert Maler's second visit to Tikal (Maler 1908, 1911).

1910

Alfred M. Tozzer and R.E. Merwin of the Peabody Museum spent twenty-three days at Tikal preparing a map to be published with Maler's report (Tozzer 1911).

1914

H.J. Spinden and S.G. Morley spent four days at Tikal (Morley 1938:56).

1921

The first of two visits to Tikal by Fernando Cruz, a Guatemalan engineer (Morley 1938:99, 268), as well as a visit by Morley, O.F. Cook, and R.D. Martin. Cook and Martin collected botanical specimens from Tikal and elsewhere in the Petén (Morley 1938).

1923

Morley, O.G. Ricketson, and several others visited the site. Most of the visitors were connected with the Carnegie Institution of Washington (Morley 1938:88–89).

1924

Ricketson and W.A. Love went to Tikal to determine its geographic coordinates (Morley 1938:89). Frans Blom visited the site (Morley 1938:90).

1927

The English archaeologist T.W.F. Gann was at Tikal (Morley 1938:81).

1928

This was an active year. There were visits by Morley (1938:90), Blom (Morley 1938:97), J. Eric S. Thompson, Edith B. Ricketson, and others (Schwartz 1990:193–200; Thompson 1954:3–11, 1963:194–201).

1930

The Englishmen—Jolly, Herron, Robson, and Stead—removed the cached offerings under Stelae 5 and 10 (Cerezo 1951) in April of that year. The next month, excavations were made beneath 12 other carved and plain stone monuments by members of a Guatemalan-Mexican boundary commission led by General Eduardo Hay, the Mexican ambassador to Guatemala, and Engineer Fernando Cruz. A.L. Smith of the Carnegie Institution's Uaxactun Project was also present and was fortunately able to take notes (Morley 1938:99, 268; TR. 27A: Appendix 8).

1931

H.H. Bartlett, based at Uaxactun, collected botanical specimens at Tikal and elsewhere in the Petén (Lundell 1937:49).

1937

A.L. Smith, H.E.D. Pollack, and E.M. Shook (Fig. L01) of the Carnegie Institution of Washington's project at nearby Uaxactun spent four days at Tikal. Shook discovered Tikal's North Zone (Morley 1938:95).

1942

Shook made a short visit to Tikal to collect data on Temple II (Str. 5D-2) (Cerezo 1951).

1948

The Guatemalan writer Carlos Jerabek visited Tikal (Jerabek 1959:18).

1951

The Guatemalan Army constructed a small airfield at Tikal, which resulted in the discovery of a few historic artifacts and an extraordinary Late Classic building whose roof comb was carved with hieroglyphs. This temple is designated Str. 6F-27 on the Tikal Map and is also referred to as Temple VI or The Temple of the Inscriptions (Berlin 1951).

Early 1950s

After the construction of the airfield, there were frequent visits to Tikal. During the first part of the decade, several North American companies began prospecting for petroleum in the Petén. Tikal was included in the Esso concession. The area was mapped for Esso by the Petty Geophysical Company, which cut numerous trails through the rainforest. These trails, or *brechas*, later facilitated mapping survey (TR. 11:1).

1956

The Tikal Project of the University Museum of the University of Pennsylvania established its field camp near the Tikal Aguada in preparation for extended excavations at the site, which continued until 1969.

Appendix F

Letter from Edwin M. Shook to Hattula Moholy-Nagy

Harvard, Massachusetts
February 6, 1962

Dear Hattula,

In 1956 when we began to clear the forest and the ground surface on the aguada ridge where the present camp stands, we found manos, flint choppers, potsherds, glass bottles and fragments, tin cans, etc. Some of this material was saved under Op. 1A, Lot 1, and 1D, Lot 4, the latter thought to be from the 19th century settlement. A similar lot, 1D, Lot 2, was found together beneath the roots of the huge *cedro* [Spanish cedar] tree, dead, fallen and accidentally burned in 1956, the charcoal stump of which still stands on the south edge of the road about where the electric power line crosses the road below my house.

The same season as workmen searched for palm thatch for building materials nearby, they found a fair amount of surface material along the slope where the present toilets are located and also throughout the now cleared area of the hotel. Note the number of old bitter orange trees around the hotel. This is 1D, Lot 1. Also, on top of the mound on the right-hand of and nearest the path leading to Tono's hotel toilets, was the material in 1D, Lot 9. Both Tono Ortiz and Vivian [Broman] de Morales may remember these finds.

The metal bell was not found by Project workmen, but by one of the government airfield workmen, Sr. Rafael Caseres, around 1950 when the government was opening the original airfield at Tikal and the workmen lived in *champas* [lean-tos of poles and palm fronds] just below our commissary building. Sr. Caseres describes having found it in the bush, some distance S. W. of the aguada. From his description, I believe it came from around the cluster of 19th century remains in the west-central area of Sq. 5F. I heard of the bell and traced down Sr. Caseres in Guatemala City and he very kindly donated it to the Tikal Project for the Tikal Museum.

Coronel Ramiro Gereda Asturias, in 1957, discovered a bayonet near the Uaxactun trail about where the road to E Group [Gp. 4E-4] takes off. He believed that it belonged to a 19th century type of gun. He did not turn in the bayonet to the Project but kept it as a memento. Col. Asturias is at present Guatemala Ambassador to Santo Domingo.

I found the house site in 1956, marked on Sq. 5F at E200 S268, where there are wild orange trees and two non-Peten type palm trees [RS 5F-3]. No remains of the house were visible, but there were stones of the fireplace, pots and stone mortars sitting around (color photo here in Harvard), fragments of chinaware, and a broken pot covering the very rusty remains of a machete blade (1D, Lot 7). E.M.S. diary, March 18, 1956. "One low group of mounds had remains of a modern (1870±?) camp with stones for fireplace, red water jars, ollas, and bowls, half of a machete blade and several stone mortars." The following year, 1957, Jim Hazard [1957:24, 25, 42] mapped Sq. 5F and ran into the other locations shown on the map. He found the masonry foundation shown at E65 S310 and the metate (1D, Lot 6) which Guillemin later fitted to Stela 21. The symbols [an open circle bisected by a short horizontal line] locate pottery finds (1D, Lots 5, 7, 8) or other evidence of the 19th century settlement. The three circles, 1–3, shown as chultuns are circular depressions which should be investigated. These probably are not chultuns.

The area with individual large stones suggesting possibly a cemetery lies 60 m. N. W, of Str. 5F-27. A careful search of this general area after light bushing seems warranted. I have not been there since Hazard was mapping. Pancho Avila, Ramon Lopez, Alfredo Kuylen, and Felipe Lanza all worked with Jim Hazard in that area and they may be able to help you.

The locations of Wurman's 1958 find (1D, Lot 10) and Gregersen's in 1960 (1D, Lot 11) are given on the Op. cards.

The corn-grinder and machete found in 1961 came from Sq. 7E, at approximately E480 S360, east of Aguada Corriental and pertain to the *Chiclero Phase!*

Sherds from the 19th century settlement (1D) should be in the laboratory on the rafter shelves, S. side, directly above the stationery supply shelves. Vivian handled most of this material.

Let me know how you make out with this interesting problem. Ginny joins in sending best regards.

As ever,

Ed

Edwin M. Shook

Appendix G

Letter from Dennis E. Puleston to Hattula Moholy-Nagy

Antioch College Union
Yellow Springs, Ohio
October 31, 1963

Dear Hattula,

[...]

First of all about the tree. Soon after arriving in Tikal this summer, I went down to take a look at your excavations in Square 5F and while there found a new chultun about 12 meters north of the center of Str. 5F-27. This new chultun I later excavated and at that time became aware of the presence of the tree by way of its small coconuts which were scattered about on the ground around the chultun. I asked the men about it and Manuel Santiago was the one who told me it grew only in the savannah areas south of Flores. Judging by the approach and approximate location of the tree you say Tono [Antonio Ortiz] showed you I would say that this tree was the other one you mention. Its actual location is about 15 meters NE of the chultun (Ch. 5F-4) which I have already mentioned. The tree, about 100 feet high, is definitely a palm judging by the palm-like fronds and the fact that it produces coconuts. I had expressed the desire to climb the tree but was discouraged by the men who pointed out rows of very long black spines which line the edges of the bases of the leaves and apparently serve to prevent just such endeavors. This feature was pointed out to me on fronds which had fallen to the ground. Judging from the coconut palms which I am familiar with in the South Seas I would say that this tree was 50 to 100 years old.

I found no other 19th century material in Square 5F but on another trip out to the rather remote Aguada Sub-in (Square 4B), in the area indicated as the site of evidence of 19th century settlement, I found a series of hearths (3 stone type) and a large biscuit tin which though well rusted looked more 20th than 19th century to me. I later took Bill H. [Haviland] out to this place and perhaps he has already given you this information. I think he would agree with me in saying this is more probably an early 20th century chiclero camp. [...]

Best regards,

[Denny]

Notes on San José Material Culture of the Late 1950s–Early 1960s

Information from Rubén E. Reina, 5 December 1961 and 9 December 1961
University of Pennsylvania Museum, Philadelphia

Notes of 5 December 1961

HOUSES

Walls of vertical poles and mud with whitewashed plaster.

Guano (thatch palm) roofs are traditional, but now some houses have corrugated metal roofs.

Tamped earth floors.

The doorway, usually facing east, often has two steps that are made of split logs held in place by stakes, the same method used on trails at Tikal.

Sometimes there are two doorways. The second is lined up with the first and leads out to the kitchen.

Traditionally there were no windows in the houses.

The kitchen is a separate structure [Fig. L27].

Cooking is done on a built in platform on an iron griddle over the fire [Fig. L27]. They do not use pottery *comales*. Reina thinks that perhaps the locally available clay is not suitable.

CHURCH

It is constructed like the houses, but has a plastered floor. Reina was told that in former times the plaster was mixed with beeswax.

Black beeswax candles are used in the church (and should leave traces on the floor).

The altar is towards the back of the church.

PIBIL

A pit oven or *horno,* ca. 2 x 1 x 1.5 m. Heated stones are placed in the bottom, a pig's head then put in and covered with hot stones. (Charred stones might be an archaeological indicator of such an oven.)

FIELDS

Often there is a raised platform for the temporary storage of maize ears, usually on six legs made of forked tree limbs. The presence of such platforms might be recognized by lime beneath them. Lime is sprinkled over the ears in the belief that it blinds the rodents who try to eat them.

HOUSEHOLD INVENTORY

Locally made wooden furniture: three-legged low tables and low wooden chairs, perhaps a Yucatecan trait, as well as regular-sized chairs and four-legged tables [Fig. L27].

Hammocks of Yucatecan type (twined?). Now they are also made of denim.

Iron meat hooks.

As a light source, a bottle filled with kerosene and used with a wick.

Bottles are also used as fish traps. The base of the bottle is removed and the bottle placed in the water neck downwards. A tortilla is used as bait. [At Tikal in 1974 I saw a fish trap made of a large rectangular tin with a rope handle and many perforations in the base. Tortillas were used as bait.]

Fish spears of cane with a forked arrangement made of umbrella ribs at the business end.

Troughs for feeding animals dug out of logs, like the *canoas* [boats].

A beam balance made of wood with pans of *jicara*

[gourd]. Domestic and ritual uses of jicaras:

Whole gourds are used like jars [Fig. 8].

Halved gourds are used like dippers and cups.

Sawed off bases, shaped like shallow bowls, used only in religious ceremonies to hold offerings of food [Fig. L28].

Kerosene cans used for storing *atole* [Note: maize gruel].

Large pottery wide-mouthed jars shaped like chamber pots (ollas) with recurved sides and flattish bottoms used to store atole, water [Figs. 14a, c-f, L27]. These jars do not have handles.

Cooking is now done in enameled metal ware [Fig. L27], as in Mexico, except for religious ceremonies, when the cooking is done in pottery vessels [Fig. L26].

Also now eat from enamelware [Fig. L28].

Edibles are stored in nets and trays suspended from the ceiling against rodents [Fig. 8, L27].

Metates are no longer used, but Reina saw an old one that belonged to the great-grandmother of his 65-year-old informant. It was massive, of the tripod type with one support at the highest end [cf. Fig. 12] and had a strongly concave grinding surface indicating heavy use. The stone was not local. There was no associated mano. In April, 1964, Rafael Morales bought this metate for the Tikal Museum.

Slide Viewing of 9 December 1961

ARCHITECTURE AND SETTLEMENT PATTERN

Elevation of a house showing two windows, each placed near the corners. The doors are usually somewhat off-center, usually to the left.

A couple of aberrant examples: one with the doorway facing west, and one with the door on the short [i.e., end] wall. Reina said that this latter house was built by a family that is not from San José.

In plan, one end is slightly rounded like the apsidal houses of Yucatán.

There are two types of wall finishing: The older type of house only has interior plastered walls. The newer ones have whitewashed plaster on the interior and exterior walls.

There is stone chinking around the heavier window and door beams. At times also between upright poles.

Long transverse poles within the houses to reinforce the walls. Sometimes find only one such pole, at about the middle height of the wall. If there are two, the upper one is at the level of the window sill.

The house walls are set on stone foundations. And there are also a few courses of stones on the exterior.

Characteristic piles of stones around houses in the fields. Stones have all kinds of uses, including cooking.

Maize ears are stored in the husk on platforms in the houses.

Some of the houses have fences of poles around them. The younger generation favors fences more than the older one.

Their drinking water comes from springs. Lake water is used for other purposes.

Irregular settlement pattern. There are houses up on the ridge (*arribas*) and houses farther down the slope (*abajas*).

The houses of San José are set well back from Lake Petén Itzá even though there is well-drained, level land more conveniently located.

Watch for cemeteries around Tikal. They are usually on high places where there is not a lot of vegetation, where the ground is easy to dig. In San José the house nearest the cemetery is about two blocks away from it. Wooden crosses with tin shelters are used to mark the graves.

Note on chiclero camps, which Reina suggests as the possible origin of some of the Recent material found at Tikal and how to distinguish camps from aldeas and villages archaeologically:

The buildings in a camp tend to be aligned.

Camps consist of more rudimentary constructions than a village. There are no walls or foundations, therefore, the floors are of a different nature. The roofs are broader, extend farther, the rooms are wider.

Generally there is a large house in which the chicle is cooked (look for charcoal) and smaller houses for sleeping. Chicleros sleep on somewhat raised wooden platforms.

In 1895–1897 they began to talk about exploiting Petén chicle, but the first chiclero camps were not established until the 1920s.

AGRICULTURE AND PLANTS

The people of San José have their *milpas* (cornfields) at some distance from their homes, and therefore build temporary shelters in the fields.

Swidden agriculture. Each man generally owns four fields. Each field is divided into two parts. One part is planted for two seasons in a row, then left fallow for eight years. At the end of eight years apparently full fertility is restored. There is no use of fertilizer. After burning, the fields are not cleared and, in fact, they are used as sources of firewood by the farmers.

Banana trees are not harmed by burning. People say that fire helps them.

It is possible to tell how old a field is and what it has been used for by the color of the smoke.

They plant while the ground is still warm and humid, i.e., while the earth "sweats." They do some weeding, but cannot keep up with it.

Of help at Tikal would be the presence of foreign plants. Reina suggests talking to Tono about this. E.g., watch for sugarcane. The presence of native *ramón* (breadnut) trees (*Brosimum alicastrum*) should also be noted. The nuts are used to make tortillas in times of food shortage. There was an example of such use at the Lake during a famine in 1903.

Special "black" corn, actually a deep reddish brown, is grown to make tortillas in the Day of the Dead (November 1st) rituals.

(Aerial photographs of Tikal might also be of help in locating old cornfields.)

There are coconut trees in San José and Flores. People don't use it efficiently and usually sell the nuts. Whoever plants a tree owns it, even if it is on someone else's land.

As in Mexico, flowers are very important in religious ceremonies. Use of the *flor de mayo* [*Plumeria* spp.]. Generally they mount the blossoms on palm stems and make arrangements of them.

POTTERY MAKING

Pottery vessels are made by hand of local clays [Fig. L26]. [In 1962, a woman potter I talked to in San José was impressed at the thinness of the walls of pre-Columbian pottery vessels. Due to use of ash temper?]

The pottery vessels are fired very slowly, in contrast to Chinautla potters who fire quickly using straw fuel. First the pots are preheated slowly on and around an open fire. Then they are placed in the fire and covered up and cooked for about an hour. Then they are taken out of the fire to cool. Potters put hot stones in the pots so that they will cool more slowly. Perhaps this is due to some peculiarity of the local clay.

MISCELLANEOUS

Matracas [wooden noise-makers] are only used during Holy Week to call people to church.

Regarding the three skulls kept in the church at San José: the Cocom families in Yucatán also had a skull (*calavera*) cult.

Beeswax is used for candles in religious ceremonies and also as an adhesive. Reina showed a photo of model planes made by boys of sticks and balls of beeswax.

Long wooden molds are used for making cakes of *panela* (brown sugar).

Carrying net made of knotted rope, slung over one shoulder. Not much use of tumplines.

Slingshots are used by boys to shoot birds. They are quiet.

Bottles are reused to carry water, like the Tikal workmen do. Used as canteens.

Women like to wear a lot of jewelry. They used to wear the Yucatán white cotton costume: a short-sleeved shift that reached to the ankles with a drawstring neck, which had a string belt at the waist. Over this they wore a short-sleeved, square-necked *huipil* (overblouse), reaching almost to the knees. The neckline of the huipil had an embroidered border in black cross-stitch. Occasionally an old woman will wear such an outfit, but the government has discouraged it for ca. 60 years.

Canoas, dugout boats, are made of mahogany (*caoba*). They are made in the forest and transported to the Lake in finished condition.

Appendix I

Professor Walter M. Wolfe's Trip to Tikal, 1901

This is an excerpt from the travel diary of Prof. Walter M. Wolfe (Fig. L24}, Brigham Young University, which records his trip to Tikal, 7–16 June 1901. I transcribed this excerpt for digital publication from earlier transcripts made by Brigham Young Library, of which there are at least two, which I received through the kindness of Prof. John E. Clark and Arlene Colman, and publish here through the courtesy of Irene Adams, Reference Specialist, Special Collections, Harold B. Lee Library, Brigham Young University, Provo, Utah. Because this excerpt is, at the least, a third-generation copy of Wolfe's account, it undoubtedly includes an unknown number of discrepancies. In order to be accepted as Wolfe's own words, it should be checked against the original diary, which is in the Special Collections of the Harold B. Lee Library of Brigham Young University.

[ ] Note added by HMN
( ) in the Library transcript

Book 3, 1901 January 11–August 7

Monday, June 3, 1901
    Very tired after the jaunt of yesterday. Boils painful and uncomfortable. Telegraphic communication restored, but no word from Don Clandoves. The event of the day was the *relista* or monthly review of all those in military service. From what I had heard imagined that relista was something great. It consisted in the boys putting on their best uniforms and answering to roll call before the comandante of the plaza. The band also played—after a fashion.

Tuesday, June 4, 1901
    This morning Dr. telegraphed to Don Clandoves for the third time. My boils made me incapable of exertion, so I remained at Dr's house all day long. Mail arrived about 2 PM. Received a large package of papers from Minister Hunter, but no letters from any source.

Wednesday, June 5, 1901
    After coffee went on the rounds with Doctor R. First visited the fat old padre who had just returned from a tour of his parishes in time to collect the Corpus Christi offerings. He was full of stories of the famine and told how much work he had done and how little pay he had got for it; thence to a compadre's; thence to house of a young woman who was dying with consumption, back to padre to get him to go and confess her and administer extreme unction. He demurred because the people were poor and had not the price to pay, but finally Don persuaded him to go; thence to plaza, while at the next place was summoned up to the administrador's office. Don Trinidad Pacheco had an order from Don Clandoves to pay me $200 billetes. Great relief. Could not get any money changed today. The highest price offered was 56¢. Doc recd a telegram from Don Clandoves telling him that Don Bette would pay the money. In the afternoon I wrote to Bro. Brimhall telling him that I should start immediately for Tikal and laying down the financial difficulties. Everybody is making preparations for Corpus. Houses are being decorated with palms and ribbons, altars are being erected. In the evening stayed up until midnight visiting. Everybody kept open house—music, dancing, drinking.

Thursday, June 6, 1901
    Up at dawn and wrote to Van telling him of my plans and advising that he start soon for Guatemala.

Mailed it before 6 and stayed at plaza until 7 when I went to Dr's for coffee. About 9 the procession passed, priest, images and all. Then made round of the town. In the PM much music and dancing, at every place where there was an altar. About 4 PM Delphine (negro) came over from San Benito and I engaged him for the trip at $1 per day and board, also engaged Emiliano Vasquez to act as guide. Impossible to change any more billetes so I bought $90 in coffee @ 62-½ billete. Of this 30 billete was credited on my board bill of $31.50 sols at 18.25 sols. Paid also 2 sols on board leaving bal. of 11.25. Pd Delphine $4 for bringing my luggage from La Libertad –

   1.25   1.25   .35 washings

Bought sugar, coffee, stationery, shoes. My boils worse than at any time before. Bed about 8 o'clock. Too many boils to permit my lying comfortably—so spent a very restless night.

Friday, June 7, 1901

Up at dawn. When I went for coffee I took Bro. Brimhall's letter to the Dr. with the request that it be forwarded by the first opportunity to Belize. No more Guatemalan stamps for me until I get back to Puerto Barrios.

About 8 o'clock Delphine came over and I used him all day in powder, shot buying (flour, lard, rice, candles, salt, sausage, pepper) enough to last us a week. It was the most costly bill of goods that I have ever tackled. Doc lent me his pavilion [Note: mosquito protection] for my hammock and between his place and the Roch house I got enough dishes for the trip. Had great difficulty in getting canoe and paddles. Finally secured the former from Doña Rosalia Burges and the oars from Don Carsaino. It was 7 o'clock when we set out and we hoped to make El Remate by 3 AM, but Emiliano was paralyzed drunk and after he had paddled for about an hour he fell asleep and we could not awake him. Delphine toiled manfully until after midnight, but we had made scarcely two leagues. So he was obliged to run the boat into the bulrushes (a dark, malarious place) and we lay down on the bottom of the canoe and went to sleep.

Saturday, June 9, 1901

Delphine and I were up with the break of day, neither of us had slept much. My boils kept me from lying in any comfortable position. Had considerable difficulty in arousing Emiliano who had the big head (goma) besides being drunkenly sick. At 6 o'clock reached Don Oliguino's ranch where we stopped while Delphine cooked breakfast. Left at 7. The ride was a long and hot one, tho the day was cool compared with some that we have had in Flores. About 9 found a large, freshly killed fish (blanca) floating on the water. Only the eyes had been picked out, so Delphine cleaned and salted it. Shores heavily timbered and with low hills close to water–no ranches. Virgin forest. Heard many monkeys and other wild beasts and saw many new birds. My boils giving me much pain—several on legs and groin burst—back worst of all. Reached El Remate at 2 PM. All tired out. Emiliano half-sick and Delphine needs sleep, besides a thunder shower is threatening so we make camp for the day and take possession of an unoccupied house. Delphine got up a good dinner of blanca, rice + sausage, flour tortillas + coffee. After dinner I brought diary up to date while the boys slept in their hammocks. After writing up diary took a bath, then Emiliano went fishing and caught 4 beautiful white fish, enough for supper and breakfast. Supper at candle light. Immediately after went to bed.

Sunday, June 9, 1901

Did not rest much during the night as the boils prevented my lying comfortably in the hammock, besides I found the pavilion very close. Up at dawn and made start after breakfast, about 6:30. Emiliano borrowed gourd and three plates from the house. Took guide for about a mile as the whole country was a network of mahogany trails. Said to be only 4 leagues to water.

Emiliano followed the trail, cutting as he went. The path was imperceptible to my untrained eye. The day was extremely hot, uphill and down thru the jungle. Saw many chicle trees that had been tapped for the rubber [Note: the sap was used to make chewing gum]. Also a few chico sapotes [little sapodillas]. It was about a month too late for the first, tho we found one or two overripe chicos that seemed to quench our thirst. Once Delphine and I had a long rest while Emiliano went after some cojolites (a bird as large as a turkey + very wild) that we had scared from their feeding ground in the sapote trees. He was not successful, but an hour later he shot a *pisano*, male, that dressed from 10 to 12 lbs. Large black crest; upper plumage black; abdomen + lower tail coverts white; cere immense, bright gamboge yellow; bill not gallinaceous. He told me that the female lacks the yellow cere and had prevailing color red. This fowl made an extra load for Delphine and he vowed that he would carry no more game. In the afternoon Emiliano kept constantly losing the trail. The perspiration, for I was dripping from head to foot (even trousers + leggings soaked thru) greatly aggravated the boils on the back. The journey seemed interminable and whenever we asked E about the distance, he would reply "no muy lejos" (not very far). This was all we could get out of him. Finally D and I were obliged to stop and rest. When we caught up with E, he was sitting by the trail at forks. He had shot a deer. Left trail for Tikal and turned to water. In about 200 yds came to the deer—a doe, large and very fat, udder full of milk, shot in head but not bled. It took E over an hour to find the water (Ixtito marked *Satinta* on map). There were no signs that any other human beings had ever visited the spot. This was between 3:30 and 4 o'clock. Delphine immediately set about to prepare the *pisano,* while E went back for the deer. Before he returned the rain came up, typical, drenching, tropical shower. All hands set to work and soon we had up a palm champa (thatched roof) that kept out the rain. Ticks very annoying. In an hour it cleared off. Then came the skinning and dressing of the deer. These people regard the lungs as a great delicacy. During the skinning process another boil burst to my great relief, but the boils on the back continue obstinate. Had supper about 6, only ⅓ of the fowl was eaten and a little of the deer liver. Another shower threatened and a champa was built to protect the fire where the venison was to be roasted. Before it was half completed, the downpour came and continued all night, but the roasting went on. The deer was quartered + put on a low frame of green wood over the fire, fowl put on also. Skin stretched on sticks and put by fire to dry. All this took until about 10 o'clock. Then as we were thoroughly wet, D made us a cup of coffee to go to bed on. Naturally it kept me awake for hours. Beds on ground, used pavilion for cover. Country traveled today rich and rolling. Mahogany, vole, chicle, sapote, salsaparilla, vanilla.

Monday, June 10, 1901

Up at daylight. Cloudy and wet. The meat was left over a slow fire to remain with the hide until our return. After breakfast we took 1 venison ham + ½ of the *pisano* with us and started out. Just after leaving the champa, saw two deer. Many fallen trees, everything wet. Clothing from lack of change, perspiration + rain in horrible condition. Long for a change. Between 12 + 1 hard rain. Delphine and I have hard work to keep up. At one place where we stopped to rest, a band of little monkeys (micos) amused us with their antics and one got over our heads and dropped sticks on us. At 4 PM we struck a deserted chicle camp. Made search for water, but could find none. Traveled on, raining, camped in the bush at 6. Just at this time it cleared off so that we had no water for drinking. D built champa, while E went off with his machete and cut several immense vines, collecting the few drops of sap that fell from each (agua de bejuco). In this way, after about an hours work, he got three cups full so we had our coffee. Beds on ground, mosquitoes very troublesome. Have no idea how far we are from Tikal and the ruins. Even Emiliano does not seem to be very certain as to the trail. The whole country is cut up by chicle trails and we passed many ruins of champas, but now the season is too dry for rubber gathering, which will be resumed next month.

Tuesday, 11 June 1901

During the night there came up a hard rain and I had the boys put out all the dishes, so we had a good drink in the night and coffee water for morning. Up at daylight. For breakfast we had fried roast-venison, flour tortillas and coffee. Seven o'clock start. About 8 came to old champa ground and got water enough from a hollow tree to give us all a good drink. Just beyond this point Emiliano lost the trail. He went on to find it. D + I waited from 9 to 12 for his return. During most of this time there was a heavy rain, so we fixed a few palm leaves over us and squatted on the ground with ants, centipedes, ticks and mosquitoes. About noon E returned; said he followed the trail to Tikal, which was only a league distant. He had lost the trail several times and had seen a great deal of game. We started out and in about an hour came to Tikal. The only sign I saw of the place was one immense ruin, a hill in magnitude, tree grown + with hewn rocks sticking from the earth. We had to go a mile beyond this place to find water. On the way we passed what had once been an Indian ranch. The hut had been gone for many years but there were old *ollas* [Note:

cooking pots] lying around and oranges and lemons run wild. Some distance beyond this we came to the water hole, an old *champa* near it. The water was horrible, even after it was strained, and was fit only for coffee. Three champas were fixed up, one for me + D, one for E, and one for cocina (kitchen). Hard rain between 2 + 3. Dinner at 3—venison + rice. Then D made up some atole for supper + lay down, but E wanted him to go hunting with him so they started out about 4 o'clock. This gave me a good chance to get up with my diary. They had not been gone long when I heard two shots and an hour later two more. About 6 they returned—each carrying a large wild hog (jabalí). The first two shots had been at a gambol, which was wounded but got away. Then, as they were going to explore the ruins for our trip tomorrow, they ran across a drove of peccaries (about 200 in all) and killed these with two shots. These pigs were very fat. It took until after dark to get them dressed + on the roasting frame, where the lard made a bright blaze until midnight. All thru the twilight, wild turkeys (pavos) were flying and alighting about us, but we had much more meat than we could use. As soon as the pork was attended to, we took our atole, D made up the pavilion, and I turned in about 730. Emiliano complained of fever and I heard D making coffee for him during the night.

Wednesday, June 12, 1901

After a good night's rest, arose about 6:30. The first thing was to dose Emiliano with quinine. Then breakfast, when we finished the venison ham, *pisano*, and rice, leaving us the pork and flour for the rest of our trip. About 8:30 we started out for the ruins. At first we found only mound squares from 20 to 30 ft in height and about 60 ft to a side, hewn rock laid up with lime mortar. All overgrown with immense trees. Saw a large band of large, dark brown monkeys and another lot of animals eating fruit in the treetops. These "critters" looked much like our raccoons, about the same size, with bushy tails and long, pointed, white-tipped noses. They are called *pisotes*. The ruins that we passed were not the main ruins so D and I sat down for an hour while E went off to search for them. When he called I saw a grander sight than I had imagined. A pyramidal mound of hewn rock, with a base of probably 200 ft, rising to a height of upwards of 75 ft [Note: almost surely Great Temple III, Str. 5D-3,

Figs. 6, 7]. On the top of this a square buildng 20 to 30 ft in height, 25 x 20 in area. The total height would be about 100 ft. With difficulty, climbing by trees + creepers, we reached the summit of the pyramid and then had a hard + perilous search for the entrance. The walls of the upper house seem to be very hard kiln-burned brick covered with a white cement. The entrance was 10 ft wide x 8 ft high. The interior was finished in a hard, smooth, white plaster and the partition walls were a lime cement and not rock.

The double cross, as found at Mitla in the recently discovered underground chambers, is very plain here. Rooms A + C run up to an apex ^ but the connecting hall B is roofed with thick hewn + squared chicle [Note: zapote] logs, highly decorated with carvings. From the entrance the view was magnificent. Below lay a level plaza of some 40 acres, heavily overgrown with trees and dense tropical vegetation, but none of the trees reached to the level of the top of the pyramid. Opposite, across the plaza, were two similar pyramids close together, the white crowning houses rising above the green and standing out boldly against the blue of the sky. Beyond these an unbroken mass of rolling green stretched away toward the tip of Yucatán, but there was no sign of any higher ground than that on which we were standing. All the portals of these houses faced the plaza. The descent was much more difficult than the ascent.

Then E + I went to investigate another house while D searched the plaza for three pillars [stelae], covered with hieroglyphics, which the Indians claim gave their history. When we had climbed up to the second house, we heard D call and I answered him. Here I satisfied myself that the pyramids were hollow and contain rooms, but as we had nothing with which to dig, what these rooms contain must be left to some other person to find out.

The second house was a trifle smaller than the first and the chicle ceiling was more highly decorated. Shape the same. This house had been visited by the Guatemalan soldiers when they came here against the Indians in 1879. They left some names on the plaster. Here we disturbed many great bats—as large as crows.

It took a long time to get down and when we reached the bottom we called but could get no answer from Delphine. Then we started in to search for the three pillars and hunted for two hours. There was no sign of them, though the vegetation was so dense that we might at times have been within 10 ft of them. We saw in all 8 of the large houses and I should judge not less than 25 other ruins. The total area of the ruins is not less than a square mile and possibly much more. About 3 o'clock I suggested that we return to the champas, which was a league away, and now E got bewildered and could not find his way out of the labyrinth. As we were traveling about, I noticed a very peculiar and pungent odor. E told me that it came from a drove of wild hogs (jabalí). Finally I told the guide to go east and keep going east. In spite of his compass, he was describing a series of circles and always coming back to the same spot. Going east we soon reached the trail or the blaze that we had made in the morning. About 5 reached camp. We supposed, as we could get no sign or answer from Delphine, that he had returned to camp, but he was not there. Evidently the poor fellow is lost in the brush. Went down for water and saw a pair of beautiful and brilliant turkeys (pavos), which did not seem at all disturbed by our presence. Saw many new, beautiful birds in the trees, also the largest serpent I have ever seen—about 10 ft long and thick as my leg. E killed it with a long pole. He said that it was venomous, but from the shape of the head I should rather take it to be a constrictor of the python kind. E put on some pork to boil and kneaded the bread. Then he started out to search for D. It was now 6 o'clock and thundering. The afternoon had been remarkably clear. Baked bread and ate my solitary supper. Felt very weak and suffered from diarrhea. At dusk the rain began to fall. I put down my pavilion, made bed, and turned in. Later E returned without D, ate his supper, and turned in also. Heavy rain up to the time when I fell asleep.

Thursday, June 13, 1901

The rain continued all night. At daybreak I was awakened by Emiliano, who had made coffee. He immediately started in search of Delphine, leaving me alone at camp. I got my breakfast and proceeded to straighten up things. The morning was cloudy with several dashes of rain. Everything is soaking wet. My clothing is literally rotting from the heat and damp. It is decidedly offensive. The shoes, which I got only a week ago, are coming to pieces. There is a horrible odor from the offal of the hogs that were dressed on Tuesday night. Of course we expected to get away from here this morning, and when we left Flores we expected to return there by this evening or tomorrow morning at latest.

Have hardly ambition to write, but must do something to drive off melancholia.

About 1:30 Emiliano returned. He had gone all about the ruins and encircled them, but could not find where D had made his exit. However, he had located one of the pillars, which was very good news for me. After a hearty lunch, we both returned to the ruins. The pillars were not, as they had been described, near the center of the plaza, but were at the base of one of the principal pyramids—twelve pillars in one place and one solitary. There are probably many more than these thirteen.

These pillars evidently belong to two distinct epochs. Eight are of squared stone and the hieroglyphics are scroll-shaped, in curves, with a few cuneiform characters. These seem to me to be the more modern. Four of the pillars stand like this:

Eight feet high, four feet wide, and about nine inches thick. Of course they are much worn by the elements and are moss-grown, but the hieroglyphics seem to be cartouched like the Egyptian. One of them I managed to copy:

The characters are entirely different from any that I have seen before and are very illegible. Some of the pillars have fallen and it was from one of these that I got the character. In front of each pillar is a flat, round stone [altar], like a millstone, about 4 ft in diameter. I believe that these, too, have been covered with characters, but now they are moss-grown and I cannot tell whether the marks are due to weathering or to human agency.

When we returned to camp I commenced a letter to Sister Crandall. Had some excellent fried cakes for supper, made by adding salt, sugar, and lard to our flour and water. Went to bed at dusk.

Friday, June 14, 1901

We were up with the dawn, and after breakfast divided the loads. I told E that from now until we returned to Petén I would pay him $1.50 per day. We took everything except Delphine's clothing, blanket + hammock. I carried all my personal effects + sugar and salt. My load probably weighed 40 lbs. On account of boils, could not carry it on my back, but on my side, half from one shoulder and half from the other. Made first-rate time until noon, when the water gave out and I gave out, too. Found a few chico sapotes on the road and they were quite refreshing. Feet badly scalded and very painful, could go but a few yards at a time in the afternoon, but fortunately there was very little clearing to be done and it was a great relief to feel that every step from now on is nearer home. The Ultima Thule of the long campaign has been reached and is now behind us. Reached Xtacito around 4:30. Could easily have made it by 3 o'clock if I had not been so completely done for. Found the venison beginning to spoil. It could have been saved had we reached here yesterday. I was too tired to do ought but rest. E got a good supper and prepared the heart of a palm for frying for breakfast. He swung his hammock, but I was perfectly content to rest on the ground.

Saturday, June 15, 1901

Up at usual time. Hard rain during night, everything soaked and dripping. Made 7 o'clock start. My feet were even worse than they were yesterday, but boils a great deal better. Reached El Remate about 1 PM. The place was deserted. Our canoe and oars were gone. After dinner as rain threatened, we moved everything to a house that had just been vacated, and then took a bath and I washed all my "duds." The *casa* (house) where we took up our abode was so infested with fleas that after trying to endure the place for an hour we gave up in disgust and returned to the house where we had slept just a week ago. Of course our bedding and clothing were full of vermin and I hung all my things up on the fence, took another bath, and picked all that I could from my underwear. During the morning I had an opportunity to observe a female *pisano*. It is not red, as I had been told, but a grayish mottle underneath and the crest seems browner than does that of the male.

While I was taking a bath, E made an oar and located a small "tipsey" canoe. In it we shall try to make our escape tomorrow. For supper we had atole de harina (*harina* is wheat or corn flour), immediately after which I retired.

Sunday, June 16, 1901

The fleas in the blanket prevented sleep and after a long and weary night was ready to get up with the dawn. About 6:30 we started out in the crazy canoe, and after traveling something over a league, found our heavy canoe coming back from Petén with two men in it and a broken oar. Cargoes were quickly transferred and as I write we are on our way, slowly but surely. About 1 o'clock we reached the ranch of Don Oliguiro, where we stayed until about 2:30, enjoying a good lunch and coffee. I added considerably to Mother Crandall's letter during the day. The afternoon ride on the lake was threatening; thunder, black clouds, high winds. Reached Flores at 5. Went immediately to the Dr.'s. Great excitement over disappearance of Delphine. Arrest threatened. Make formal report to the *jefe*. [Note: A rescue party found Delphine at El Remate on 19 June 1901.] Receive two pkgs of papers from Mr. Hunter and 1 letter from M.R.W. Sleep at Dr.'s. Heavy rain during the night.

Appendix J

Research on the Bottles of Tikal by Paul S. Newton

People's Savings Bank
Main and State Streets
Bridgeport 1, Connecticut

August 20, 1963

Miss Hattula Moholy-Nagy
The University Museum
University of Pennsylvania
33rd and Spruce Streets
Philadelphia 4, Pennsylvania

Dear Hattula,

As promised, I enclose copies of the two letters I wrote to Ed Shook regarding the "Bottles of Tikal." The deletions mentioned in my previous letter do not affect the pertinent information contained in the original correspondence. The letter dated August 22 is certainly the better of the two.

You have my permission to publish either or both of these letters. If that is what you have in mind, they must appear in the present form: that is, as letters to Mr. Shook under dates written.

I have just discovered that my secretary addressed my last letter to you, <u>Mr.</u> Hattula! As Trudy Blom would say, "dot's tu-r-r-rable!" You owe me one addressed <u>Miss</u> Newton...

Pete joins me in sending you our best—

Paul

Paul S. Newton, Vice President

PSN:cd
Enclosures 2

May 20, 1960

Mr. Edwin M. Shook
Tikal, Guatemala

Dear Ed:

During our visit to Tikal in February you showed my wife, Pete, and me two bottles which had come to light during excavation of the site. One, a two-mold bottle bearing the name "Agua De La Reina, John H. Williams & Company, New York," in raised letters on the surface [Fig. 22c], appeared to be quite old. The other was a comparatively modern beer bottle with raised lettering indicating the name of the brewery to be Welz & Zerweck Brewery, Brooklyn, New York [Fig. 22f].

You asked us to try to get some information on these very un-Maya objects. We agreed because it seemed a simple enough task at the time. Now, after having gone through tons of data, I'm not so sure.

To begin with, the beer bottle appeared to present no problem at all as the date you gave us, 1928, is still a time within the memory of a great many people still living. I remember this period well—the Prohibition Era—Al Capone, illegal stills, etc. Pete and I searched micro-filmed New York City business and brewery directories from 1900 to 1928 in the New York Public Library. Although results so far have been negative, we are by no means discouraged. We'll begin a new search, but instead of concentrating on your 1928 data, we're going back to about 1875.

We spent most of our time on the "Agua De La Reina" bottle. The New York Public Library was very patient and helpful in supplying us with great masses of material.

Using 1845 as a starting date, we searched the New York Mercantile Union, New York and Brooklyn Partnership, New York and Brooklyn Co-partnership, shipping, and general business directories. Slowly but surely, pieces of a picture began to appear. The picture is not yet complete but I feel confident that the missing parts will be found.

Trow's New York City Directory, complete on micro-film, proved to be our best source of information. From the very beginning, 1845, the name, John H. Williams, occurred regularly in connection with the glass business but John H. Williams & Company, the name on the "Agua De La Reina" bottle, appears only during the period 1858–1859. Here is how it is listed:

John H. Williams & Company
(George H. Williams, Jr.)
7 Coenties Slip, New York City
Produce.

Two other glass concerns which had been in business since before 1850 are also listed 1858–1859:

John H. Williams & Son
(George H. Williams)
315 Pearl Street, New York City
Glass, mostly plate, retail

Williams, Stevens, and Williams
(John H. Williams, Linus Williams, George H. Williams)
Glass, plate, etc., manufacturers and importers.

You will note that John H. Williams & Company is in the produce business, a far cry from glass. It is of utmost significance, however, that its principal is George H. Williams, Jr. Apparently George, Jr. is the son of George H. Williams, the principal of John H. Williams & Son, who in turn, is the son of John H. Williams. Furthermore, John H.

Williams and his son, George, are two of the principals of Williams, Stevens & Williams, a company which manufacturers [sic] and imports glass, plate, etc. The strong family relationship which existed between the principals explains how a produce company and two glass companies can be tied together and also offers a plausible explanation as to who manufactured the bottle and for whom it was fabricated.

During our search, we tried to find information relating to trade goods and practices during the period 1850 to 1875 in order to try to identify the original contents of the bottle and find a logical reason for its appearance in the Central America area. Classified ads appearing in directories indicate that cologne or toilet water was never given a trade name using the English word, "water." Usually some sort of French caption was used with the French word for water, "eau," appearing commonly. In the 1800s, carboys of toilet water were shipped to this country from Europe where the contents were transferred to small bottles for marketing under a variety of trade names. It is likely that "Agua De La Reina" was cologne, evidently bottled for a Spanish-speaking market otherwise the trade name would have been in French...to indicate an imported product which would place it among the holy of holies in the U. S. A. marketplace of those days. However, if the product had been bottled for shipment to, say Mexico, for example, a New York import would rate far higher than one from France as that country was then having a little friction with Mexico.

If all this doesn't bore you, let's look at the market possibilities. It is a fair assumption that John H. Williams & Company bottled the "Agua" in New York City with the intention of exporting it to a Spanish-speaking country other than Europe. On the east coast, the likeliest market would be in this hemisphere somewhere north of Brazil. It is doubtful that the Spanish-speaking area in northern South America would have provided a sufficient market. Two factors pretty well rule out the Spanish-speaking countries along the west coast of South America: the Panama Canal had not yet been built and there were few significant ports. There remain, then, Central America, Mexico, the islands in the Caribbean and, in the U. S. A., the southwest and California. All this helps to establish the product as being toilet water. Most of this area normally has a hot climate and is subject to long dry seasons. I mention this because I am reminded of New Guinea. The natives there have ample opportunity to bathe but don't. I remember getting whiffs of those aborigines and frankly, a case of toilet water would have been a godsend!

"La Reina," of course, means the queen, but the only queen I can think of who was in the above area during this general period was Carlotta of Mexico (about 1864 to 1869). There is a possibility that Carlotta is "La Reina" but I'm inclined to think not. Both "king" and "queen" have been freely used in trade names.

You will note that the business of John H. Williams & Company was designated in the directory simply as "produce," a business which appears to have no connection with toilet water. In those days, the produce business may have encompassed a broader scope of activities than its present-day counterpart which is highly specialized. On the other hand, the very nature of John H. Williams & Company's business may have led it into exporting toilet water. Located on Coenties Slip on the East River in lower Manhattan, it was in the very heart of international shipping. Close by, relatives of George H. Williams, Jr., the principal, were successfully manufacturing as well as importing glass. It doesn't take much imagination to see how, observing the unloading of carboys of toilet water from ships in the vicinity of Coenties Slip, they got the idea to use their established facilities to import the "Agua" in bulk, mold their own bottles and handle exportation of the rebottled product through John H. Williams & Company. This would work out fine for John H. Williams & Company because a cargo of "Agua De La Reina" would provide a means of exchange for produce and thereby offset the expense of deadheading to some Mexican or Central American port.

This concludes the first installment of the "Bottles of Tikal." What we hope to accomplish next is a complete story on the Welz & Zerweck bottle. We will also complete our search on the "Agua De La Reina" bottle.

You and your staff helped make our visit to Tikal a very enjoyable one. Pete and I found the route from British Honduras to Tikal very exciting and interesting. We hope to do it again next year.

Cordially,

Paul S. Newton
80 Cartwright Street
Bridgeport, Connecticut

August 22, 1960

Mr. Edwin M. Shook
Little Common
Harvard, Massachusetts

Dear Ed:

To continue with the "Bottles of Tikal."

Pete and I have found this project to be a complete and welcome change of pace, although the time I have had available to devote to it has been seriously restricted by having to earn a living and similar minor distractions. I have also felt obliged to devote some portion of my time to such exciting activities as: "Beautify Bridgeport," neighborhood improvement, "Down With Blight," redevelopment, et cetera, all of which have taken on new meaning—and urgency!—since seeing what happened to Tikal.

Whether or not our bottle research will be of any value to you, it at least has provided Pete and me with a vast wealth of useless information. For example: The first crown bottle cap was invented by William Painter in 1892; the first automatic glass bottle molding machine was patented by M. J. Owens in 1895; New York City had a yellow fever epidemic in the early 1800s; the amount of air occupying the free space in the neck of a bottle of beer when it is capped tremendously affects its shelf life, particularly with regard to flavor and brightness; until quite late in the 1800s, cigars were called Segars; et cetera ad infinitum. Notwithstanding the constant temptation to become sidetracked by these fascinating gems, we at long last completed our work on the "Bottles of Tikal."

To begin...we now have confirmed beyond all doubt that the John H. Williams & Company on the "Agua De La Reina" bottle is the same company as the one located at 7 Coenties Slip. I mentioned in my previous letter that for many years John H. Williams had been prominently identified with the glass business. Also, I listed three companies in existence during the years 1858 and 1859 whose principals, I assumed, were all members of the same family. On the face of it, the evidence appeared conclusive enough, but a startling discovery removed all doubt.

In early 1860, and possibly during the last half of 1859, all three companies terminated. Furthermore, all the principals with which we are concerned, John H. Williams, George H. Williams and George H. Williams, Jr. disappeared forever from the New York City Directories. What happened is anyone's guess. Possibly, old John H. died and perhaps George, Sr. and his son shipped out for, say, Central America? Supposing something of this kind actually happened, the question then arises: What specific country in Central America?

We looked through numerous books on Central America hoping the name, "Agua De La Reina," would appear somewhere or we would discover a useful clue. A traveler in Panama, writing of his experiences about 1850 in an area adjacent to the Costa Rican border, refers to "Reinas" the same way we call young ladies "chicks" or "dolls." When you're grasping at straws, almost anything is encouraging. In this case, we were encouraged by the suggestion that "Reina" would make an attractive and appropriate trade name for toilet water...at least, in Panama!

At this precise point, we decided to take another long look at George H. Williams, Jr. in the hope we could find some connection which would tie him to a specific Spanish-speaking country.

The following listing in Trow's New York City Directory appeared under [the] date of 1858:

John H. Williams & Company
(George H. Williams, Jr.)
7 Coenties Slip, New York City
H. 15 Carroll Place
Produce.

We had previously copied this from the 1859 directory in which George, Jr.'s residence address did not appear. It took but a moment to turn to Carroll Place. Opposite number 15 was this simple listing:

George H. Williams, Jr.
Merchant
H. New Granada

Zounds! New Granada at that period of history comprised all of what is now Columbia [sic] and Panama and then, as now, it was a Spanish-speaking area.

This was IT!

You can imagine the thrill of this simple discovery. It removed a pressing question from my mind and obligingly placed the bottle right down into the Central American area.

History shows the Yanks were particularly active in the region at that time. In 1858, John L. Stephens' two volumes, "Incidents of Travel, etc." were still stirring the imaginations of the restless Yanks with the release that year of the twelfth edition of his first two famous volumes. Three years before, on February 24, 1855, the Daily Courier of Aspinwall, New Granada (the Colombia district of the Government of New Granada was disrupted in 1831 and the region of Panama became known as New Granada. Aspinwall, incidentally, located at what is now the Atlantic entrance to the Panama Canal, later became the city of Colon) graphically described the inauguration of the Panama Railroad, an organization which not only wedded the Atlantic to the Pacific for the transit of passengers and goods bound to California and points west, but also whose fantastic profits over many years to follow have become legendary. Only twelve years earlier, an expedition from Guatemala City had found Tikal and now, in the year 1860, it seemed that someone else was about to put dreams into action by undertaking the long, hard trek to that jungle-shrouded city.

What, actually, do we know about our bottle?

We know with reasonable certainty the "Agua De La Reina" bottle was manufactured in New York about the year 1858 and shipped to Panama or somewhere nearby at least by mid-1860. It certainly made its way to Tikal probably by way of Belize, British Honduras, by ship, then up the Belize River to El Cayo and finally, overland by mule through the Peten rainforest to its final destination. In those days it must have been an extremely rough and difficult trip.

Anyone who has traveled in Central America knows that bottles have always been used over and over again sometimes for years and years. However, our bottle was small, quite inadequate to be of much use as a container. Also, when found it was in excellent condition, beautifully crystallized but neither damaged nor chipped.

In conclusion: A bottle of cologne, called "Agua De La Reina," original contents intact, reached Tikal not much later than 1860. Sometime before 1865, this empty container was thrown into a pit where it was discovered by archeologists almost a century later.

You might say, "Flushed with success, they then departed from what was once the Transfer Reservoir of the City of New York, now the Public Library."—But not so. There was still the case of the bottle of the beer boys, Welz & Zerweck...

In 1878, John Welz had a brewery on the corner of Myrtle and Wyckoff Avenues, Brooklyn, New York. In that year he sold 6,982 barrels of beer, a fair batch of headaches for a man who started with a single barrel 16 years before. In 1879 he sold 9,744 barrels which put him into the top half of his class. Along around 1882, John apparently couldn't count fast enough to keep track of the ever-increasing barrels leaving his brewery...or perhaps he felt the business should be doing better. At any rate he took on a partner, Charles Zerweck. Evidently, John wanted the name to be this way until all the old letter-heads were used up because it wasn't until a year or so later that the name became Welz & Zerweck. Under this name the company prospered for 37 years until that fateful day in 1920.

Welz & Zerweck were legitimate brewers, and, unable to fill their vats with the real thing, they probably resorted to making an unreasonable facsimile in the form of "ne'er beer." Either their product was inferior, even for an inferior product, or they simply became discouraged of the whole mess. At any rate, in 1928 the brewery moved from its location at Myrtle and Wyckoff Avenues, a place it had occupied for half a century, to new quarters at 36 Forrest Street, Brooklyn. Here it remained until 1932, but there is reason to doubt that the business prospered because in that year the old brewery disappears forever with the following listing: Welz & Zerweck, Real Estate, 215 Montague Street.

There you have the background of the Tikal beer bottle, but it is another matter to assign to it a precise date. The period upon which to concentrate would certainly be prior to 1920 because anything bottled after that date wouldn't be worth carting two city blocks let alone all the distance to Tikal. Furthermore, ne'er beer would not have the particular qualities assigned to real beer by those who know more about it than I do. Permit me to quote another little gem, "Explorers and travelers (in the tropics), who make frequent use of good beer, are generally healthy and preserve their color; whilst those less fortunate, who do not use beer at all, are devoured by fevers and intermittents" (so there!). This writer goes on to say that it is safer and more palatable than guzzling wine or getting crocked on brandy. Except for the part about brandy which I find singularly agreeable, I go along with the idea and I'll even go a step further by suggesting that no self-respecting explorer would be caught dead in any decent jungle in company with a bottle of ne'er beer.

The time element is thus reduced from 1882/1932 to 1882/1920 or from 50 down to 36 years. This in turn can be split almost down the middle by taking into consideration one particular characteristic in the evolution of commercial bottles—the crown cap. This divides the 36 years into (1) the early period, 1882/1900 (plus) and (2) the late period, 1901/1919 (possibly a very little earlier and no later than 1919 because the Volstead Act went into effect January 19, 1920). When found, the Welz & Zerweck bottle was in excellent condition. It was not chipped and the glass had not crystallized. It was a machine-made container of the crown cap type and probably manufactured between 1915 and 1919. It was not carried to Tikal by a Central American: if it had been, it would very likely have been carried right out again. Furthermore, we found quite good information about Welz & Zerweck but nothing to show that the company had ever exported beer to that area.

In my opinion, a well-equipped, experienced American explorer and/or archeologist shipped out of New York sometime between 1915 and 1919. He liked beer, particularly the Welz & Zerweck product. He landed in Belize, British Honduras and followed the same route to Tikal as [the] "Agua De La Reina" bottle over a half century earlier.

For our part, this concludes the "Bottles of Tikal." Pete and I hope this material will be useful to you and we look forward to another assignment.

Sincerely,

[Paul S. Newton]

Appendix K

Salvador Valenzuela's Report on the Department of Petén, 1879 (Valenzuela 1951)

Translated from Spanish by Marshall J. Becker, with corrections by Rubén E. Reina, May 1962

Report on the Department of Petén: Addressed to the Ministry of Development

Guatemala, June 1, 1879

Minister of Development

Sir:

I have the honor of bringing to your attention this report concerning the Department of the Petén, which I have recently visited at the request of the President and instructed by that office.

Whosoever takes into consideration the reports of *jefes políticos* [political chiefs] and commissioners of the government that have been issued in the past, and compares them with the following report, will find some contradictions concerning the condition in which one finds that Department, the character of its inhabitants, their customs, etc. However, be that as it may, I will report my own observations with honesty, thus complying with the instructions that I received from you to supply information about whichever matter seems worthy of calling to the attention of the Supreme Government.

Before taking up this subject, I must state that the map of the Republic is inaccurate from Cobán north, which shows that the author of the map had not sufficient information of the topography of the area north of Cobán and of the Department of the Petén.

It is some 100 to 110 leagues [1 league = 3 statute miles] from the capital to the city of Flores, and not 140 leagues as may have been calculated. The portion of the road to Cobán is well known. There one will make necessary preparations to continue the tortuous march through a great unpopulated area of more than 50 leagues in which one will not find resources other than those which can be furnished by the Indians of Chisec, some 16 leagues from Cobán. In the summer this road, like that which continues to Flores, can be easily traveled by horse; but no sooner do the rains begin, then the road is impassable, being a path hidden by the mountains and completely shaded from the rays of the sun, the retained water and the prominent roots of the trees form mires and muddy obstructions making the way impossible for traffic by horse and even endangering the life of the traveler. When all these difficulties are present, one needs 7 to 8 days to travel the road from Cobán to Flores during the summer and during a rigorous winter some 15 to 20. During this season, one needs to navigate from Tepesbatum to El Subín in small boats down the river to *La Pasión,* and from there upstream on the Río Subín, all in 16 hours to cover the 7 leagues that lie between these rivers.

This Department, in itself, more extensive than half of the rest of the Republic, is occupied by 12 communities governed by their respective *municipios* and under the *jefetura's* political chieftaincy: the first of these is in the city of Flores, situated on an island in the lake of Itzá; three are located on the western shore, and the rest to the south, of this same lake.

At a distance of 80 to 100 leagues north on the Yucatán trail are the communities of Chuntuquí, San Felipe, Concepción, Yacché, Santa Cruz, San Antonio, Tankach-Ahal, Dolores Xtanché, Santa Clara, Konguas, Silvituc, Bolon Petén, Thubucil, and Nojbecan. These 13 [sic] communities are only known by merchants traveling the road from Yucatán; their inhabitants are originally from this State, and they are refugee Indians as a result of the wars beginning in 1853. The communities were formed without the backing or protection of the government. Restless and war-ridden Indians, they are accustomed to complete freedom; and the Petén authorities had learned to fear them so that no past *corregidor* nor political chief of this period has dared to visit them, thereby exaggerating their hostile character. However, I have attempted to gather information about the situation and I have been informed that they come every year to the seat of government to report the election of *alcaldes,* the small funds collected, and even bringing insignificant sums that *ad libitum* are charged for *aguardiente,* gunpowder, and other effects that come from Belize. Some travelers informed me, moreover, that in transit through these villages, one encounters every class of aid from inns (*posadas*), very inexpensive provisions, porters to carry supplies, etc. They cultivate maize, beans, *yame,* some greens, and tobacco, which are profitably sold in Yucatán and to travelers passing through these communities. They like to raise hogs and domestic fowl, which are abundant, as well as livestock, which is scarce in these places. They maintain some commerce with Belize, where they procure clothing, arms, gunpowder, and hard liquor.

All this led me to understand that the authorities had exaggerated the risks which must be run should one try to organize these villages; and it is without doubt that an annual visit from the political chiefs, without any pomp, treating the Indians with kindness and common sense, would result in a quick, if not rapid, organization.

Probably those Indians hope that sometime the authorities will remember them; and therefore when the political chief sent a memorandum notifying them of my intended visit, they were prepared to receive me, and proceeded to clear the paths. All of this demonstrates that there is no hostility on their part against the authorities.

Turning now to the other communities, I will endeavor to report to you, Sr. Ministro, an approximate description of the actual situation and the factors that characterize them.

The city of Flores, capital of the Department, is situated at the south end of the lake. Its extent is some 8-3/4 blocks with a population of 1280. There no longer exists a single lot upon which one could build, consequently the population cannot exceed that which it is today. The national buildings and houses are roofed with palms; 11 small buildings and 1 of two stories with tin roofs were built within the last two years. Several times the town has been reduced to ashes and this calamity is constantly present due to the mass of huts. The reflection of the water and the natural warmth of earth constituted of limestone creates a temperature no lower than 26 degrees Réamur, going as high as 30 degrees R [89 to 98 degrees F].

The insufferable heat experienced there causes those not native to the area to emigrate to other communities, leaving on the island only the officials and some other transient visitors, but the attachment that the natives have to residing on the island is exceptional.

The residents of Flores, because they have always lived far from all populous centers, do not sufficiently know the enjoyment of comfort. Their activities are limited to acquiring the essentials of life and their needs are easily satisfied.

The customs of the group are simple, but the part of the population that is influential retains a curious simplicity of custom united with the defects of civilization. These influential people still live with little educational opportunities; among them a man considered knowledgeable has learned to read, write, and count; and some who have gone to Guatemala to study have not returned to reside in their community. Intoxication is not frequent among them.

One notices in the whole region submission to the law, intelligence and quick comprehension, and the desire to learn. All who have the opportunity to learn to read and write do so, and if they are able to acquire other education they take advantage of it, provided it isn't hard work.

The municipal jurisdiction of those towns has no demarcation, just as the town has no *ejidos* or properties. Up to now, not one title of property exists, everything being common land. For that reason, in concerning myself with agriculture, I shall discuss what belongs to each village.

Flores possesses a large territory formed by the peninsula of the lake and extending east to Belize. It also possesses other lands to the south on the shore of the same lake. On these large areas the inhabitants plant corn and beans, which actually do not amount to more than 1300 *cuerdas* [one cuerda = 0.971 acres] of first fruit and 50 of second. In addition, there are three *cuerdas* of banana and two of *yucca,* 11 small sugarcane fields—most of them in an area of two blocks— and a small iron sugar mill, and the rest—with 10, 15, and 20 *cuerdas*—comprising in all 12 blocks of sugarcane that are harvested at any time without worrying about which are ready and when the cane has scarcely begun to be sweet.

Additionally, some inhabitants own livestock in the surrounding plains, up to 1300 head of cattle and 230 horses. The municipality, by orders of the present political chief and overcoming by these orders a thousand obstacles, planted 4000 coffee trees last year.

By that which I have propounded, the Sr. Minister can see what the situation is of most of the population of the Department.

I will not take up much space in speaking of the other towns. On the west shore of the lake from 2 to 3 leagues by water from Flores, are the towns of San Andrés and San José. Appended to the latter is the small village of Tical, whose ruins I shall concern myself with presently. The first town has 623 inhabitants and the second 250. In the former there are some *ladinos* and the remainder of both are indigenes of the Yucatecan race, extremely intelligent and hard-working. They own hilly lands on which they cultivate generally consumed crops, and already there exist some henequen plantings. They are not much inclined to raise cattle, and usually these indigenes are destined to be servants, such as day laborers, commanded by the Peteneros. Those of San Andrés are affected by the militia and regularly and faithfully do their service in Flores.

In front of that town and about 600 *varas* [variable, but here probably about 33 inches] away is the lovely town of San Benito, with more than 200 inhabitants, most of the African race. This little town, by itself, has more industry and means of existence than the city. Men and women are hard workers. They plant corn, beans, bananas, *yucca, yame, macal,* and other things sufficient for their needs and for trade with others. Almost all raise pigs, which they do not fatten on garbage, and which they use when they are ready.

The temperature is cooler, and to pass through this town while taking some exercise is the only distraction given to the Flores employees.

To the east of the lake and along the road that leads to Belize are four other little lakes and different streams forming a long extension from the peninsula. This is the most important part of the surroundings of the lake of Itzal because it has abundant water, while the rest, at a distance of 6 and 8 leagues, although fertile, is nullified by the absolute lack of water.

Belonging to San Benito, and 8 leagues away on the road to this capital is the town of Sacluk, to which is added the village of San Rafael, with 400 and some inhabitants between the two of them. It is situated on a big plain more than 8 leagues south and north and 25 to 30 east and west, forming a circle around the lake, broken by a highland of 2 leagues. East of Sacluk and south of Flores on the same plain are the towns of Chachaclum with 350 people, and San Juan de Dios with the village of Ixpayac, composed of 235 people. On the plains of these towns are focused the interests of their inhabitants and of some of Flores that have formed its herds of livestock in the places suiting the individual, taking advantage of the little lakes called *aguadas,* from which, during the last days of summer, they drink muddy water – the people as well as the livestock.

I calculate from 10,000 to 12,000 cattle pastured on these plains. They increase each year very slowly, though their owners are not of minor intelligence. It is enough to say that there had been no occasion when some herder gave a pound of salt to his cows, to understand the slight degree of advancement of this industry. Fortunately, the necessity of drinking water at the small lakes obliges the livestock to gather and then annually they brand the calves. Regularly in the months of April and May there are deaths of animals, in addition to those eaten by jaguars, which isn't a few. But there is no way to convince those people that it is not disease but rather the bad water that causes that loss, in order to oblige them to clean the water annually and throw in salt as they are accustomed to do in Tabasco, where this method has given very good results.

The agriculture in these three towns is in the same state. In addition to their communal plantings, there are a few small ones of sugarcane and coffee. The important thing is two sugarcane plantings of three to four blocks, one situated in Sacluk and the other in the place called Tepesbatum under its jurisdiction. The coffee groves altogether comprise under 3000 trees; and a grove that I saw in Ixpayac produced two pounds per tree. In Chachaclum, the political chief ordered the planting of 2000 feet of coffee.

In these plains, like in those on the road to San Luis of which I will speak later, is a kind of large wild turkey, peculiar to the Petén, which has lately gained attention in Europe because of its uniqueness. They are hunted frequently during the early night and from midnight to dawn. They are so big that one is enough to feed a family of 12 people for a day, and have much resemblance to our common turkey. They are said to be too delicate to raise, but I gather what was missing was dedication for I still have a small one that I found domesticated in a chicken coop and transferred to this capital, where it is perfectly at home. If this bird can be domesticated in a pen, there will not be another to equal it, neither for the beauty of its plumage nor for the deliciousness of the meat for table use. Five leagues to the southeast of Flores, towards the road to Izabal, is the town of Santa Ana with a population of 400 inhabitants together with the village of Junto-cholol. In this plain, the land is more fertile, and the water for livestock more abundant, because the *aguadas* found here are larger and more common. All of the people keep livestock and not less than 2000 beef cattle are pastured there. All of the essential cereals are planted in quantity, and some henequen. In Junto-cholol are a few groves of coffee and cacao. Here begins the most important part of the Department, as we shall see in a moment.

From Santa Ana to the villages of Santo Toribio and Xarché—which together with that of San Blas form a single town—is 11 [sic] leagues, 2 through the plain of Santa Ana, 6 crossing a fertile highland with several rivers and beautiful waters, and 2 in another plain named Xarché, much more fertile than those of Sacluk, with sufficient water for livestock and a cooler temperature. Husbandry is better established than in most of the towns, although not as plentiful because of the poverty of the inhabitants, who generally devote themselves to communal plantings. In the middle of this highland, a man from Flores has established himself at the place named San Juan. This hard-working agriculturalist, with only one helper, has formed a small sugarcane plantation and small fields of coffee and tobacco, for a little personal gain. He who will

devote himself to work with better constituents may obtain fine results.

The inhabitants of these villages only plant communally, but their extensive plains could support 40,000 or 50,000 beef cattle. The soil is suited for any crop from a temperature of 21 to 22 degrees R [79 to 82 degrees F], and it is easy to export through Belize.

The plains of Xarché are 5 leagues long, and after passing a highland of 4 leagues, one arrives at the town of Dolores, the first I encountered with a river on its outskirts. Formerly populous, it has diminished little by little, until the decline stopped at 300 and some inhabitants, without understanding the causes of its decadence. Situated on a pine-covered plain capable of supporting 100,000 pastured beef cattle, with a temperature of 19 to 20 degrees R, sufficiently cool, with land favorable for all crops and abundant water, this plain is to be one of the most important in the Department.

There they cultivate, in addition to the usual fruits, cotton, chocolate, and tobacco, and for this they annually have a communal planting. This year's harvest is in the town hall and is of very fine quality.

From Dolores to Santa Barbara Machaquilá is a distance of 4 leagues, 3 of which are mountainous. Therefore, one travels uphill to reach these villages, gradually noting the increase in the fruitfulness of the land and lamenting that the day has not yet come in which these immense riches are to be exploited. Located near Machaquilá are the towns of Petensuc and Poctum, at 1 and 2 leagues, respectively, on the San Luis road. One may have lands in other places with great fruitfulness, water, etc. but I consider it difficult to find lands to surpass these. Nowhere in the Republic have I encountered similar lands, not only in fertility, nor extent of level land, nor in beautiful waters that flow in all directions, nor in brisk and healthy climate with a temperature of 15 to 17 degrees R [67 to 70 degrees F].

This plain covered with white and colored pines and fir trees of great height, among whose pastures cattle are hidden, extends from north to south as measured along the road for 5 leagues, but grows large to the east to an unknown extent that one may assume reaches all the way to Belize, because some cattle that have been sold from this area to Belize have appeared from that direction, and because some Englishmen who had been lost left this area and arrived in the English colony. Some from that same place had come down, walking two and three days, searching for cows that had strayed, and had encountered at some 30 leagues distance the camps of lumberjacks who cut pine and form huge rafts of the logs, but where they found it impossible to locate their cattle, or they encountered some from Belize of which I have previously spoken.

At the margin of the villages runs a navigable river, the Machaquilá, which flows from the Pasión, which in the summer unfortunately flows down into its sandy bed, reappearing at a distance of half a league. But the neighboring people have discovered the method of changing its course in spite of its great flow, and recover the sand with little cost.

The 500 inhabitants of this town and the surrounding villages are dedicated to raising cattle without slaughtering them, however; and to raising the staples, maize, beans, etc. In Poctum there are some gardens with coffee, cocoa, and small reed fields that give a picture of what can be grown there and invite a daring impresario seeking foreign colonies to multiply his capital in but a few years without fearing the lack of a means to export the fruit because from Xarché and from Dolores to the Belize frontier there is a level road that can be covered in three days, and by which wagons may pass in the summer, and from the frontier one may go down the river in one or two days.

The distance between Poctum and San Luis is 7 leagues, 3 leagues in the forest and 4 in the *montaña,* on a wretched road. The town, of more than 2000 indigenous inhabitants, is very similar in its ways and customs to the town of Cahabon, a town that has more commerce at distances up to 40 or 50 leagues. The road in the area that corresponds to the Department of the Petén has been recently opened and is wide and easily traveled. The indigenous population is dedicated to the customary staples and also to tobacco, which they know how to cure.

Actually a great quantity of reeds for hats is brought from San Luis, bound for Yucatán. The ease of cutting and curing this plant, which is also produced in Chachaclum, attracts one's attention because later it ought to form one of our exportable articles on a grand scale, if we take heed of it being inexhaustible in San Luis, Cahabon, and La Tinta in Verapaz, where we now know that it has been recorded that it is the same palm used by the people of those two towns to thatch their roofs.

As I have previously noted, you will observe that the towns situated between Santa Ana and San Luis, which is 34 leagues from Flores and on the roads from Cahabon and the new road that goes to Izabal, are the most important of those known in the Department of the Petén and the most worthy of calling to the attention of the Supreme Governor. These villages are not only rich and noteworthy due to the fertility of the land, but the natural products in the encompassed mountainous regions are also another fountain of riches that ought to be exploited. Sarsaparilla, oilcloth, balsam, vanilla, various kinds of resins, reeds for hats, and furniture of different colors and classes, etc., are to be found in these mountains, and also in the mountains of other villages and those on the road to the capital and along the banks of the Pasión River and its tributaries, and of the San Pedro, where we should cut logwood and woods of all types that appear to be inexhaustible there.

One should note that in the jurisdiction of Poctum there may be a rich silver mine that the members of the Castilian family who discovered it do not desire to explain. This was noted in Belize, and various Englishmen have made expeditions to search for it. Attention to this matter remains in the care of the political chief with definite results expectable.

I have greatly extended the relating of this information, but I believe it necessary in order that the Supreme Governor may form a more accurate opinion regarding the Department of the Petén and what is to be expected from it; and in spite of how tiring this information may be, I see the necessity of extending it to include other points of interest to the Department and for the national good.

It has not been long since the taxes of that Department were so sparse that they did not equal the salaries of the personnel, because of failure to pay taxes and through other motives.

Recently things have been changing, thanks to the appointments of political chiefs and administrators who are not native to those places; and although these persons maintain a constant battle with the few people of those parts who have a desire to resist progress, they have managed to initiate some reforms that cannot fail to be annoying to some of the people.

This year there has been a surplus of some $4000 to $5000 [Guatemalan pesos, from 1859–1925] in taxes, in spite of the increased expenses, and this surplus should be duplicated each year if intelligent and active political chiefs in accord with the administrator continue the perseverance and energy on the road to reform, which should renew the Department as the richest in the Republic.

In Flores there exists a small school teaching the art of making reed hats that, with your advice, was established by the local political chief. They managed to assemble six students with difficulty, even with threats. One of these has left, having profited from the teaching.

The teacher is one of the most intelligent in such office, and understands that the government is spending a useless salary each day that this is taught in the Petén, since only two or three will profit from the knowledge, and how with very little extra one could manage to introduce the same industry in Guatemala, for men and women, engaging the teacher mentioned here to the ends that you will see in the attached document, who would come to establish classes of hat-making in the art schools and the hospital of this city. I do not doubt but that this industry might become general among us, and that later we could see to the export of this article that is now manufactured.

The principal income is from the products of wood-cutting and from the sales tax on items that are imported from Belize, which I will treat separately.

To give some idea of the end products of wood-cutting I will relate to the Minister a story of the rivers on which the camps are situated and the means used to check them.

The river known as La Pasión originates in a place called Santa Isabel, on the road from San Luis to Cahabon, and in a few leagues its many tributaries make it deep and navigable. It takes the name "Canquen" from its origin to a distance of some 12 to 15 leagues, where it merges with the Machaquilá. From there it continues with the name of La Pasión, in a course of 60 to 70 leagues, from the southeast to the northwest to its merging with the Chisoy, crossing the entire south of the Department and receiving numerous additional tributaries. From the mouth of the Chisoy the river is known as the Usumacinta. The Usumacinta continues quite broad to a certain point in Tabasco, where it divides forming the Grijalba River with one arm and sending the other to the Laguna de Terminos. The exportation of woods from the Petén regularly passes through the port of Frontera.

Some families from Tabasco have settled in the Petén, establishing logging camps along the banks of the Pasión from which they export great quantities. In 1872 they were obliged to pay a modest tax to the political chief, Don Martín Quezada, a tax they attempted to avoid by hiding the wood they had cut. In 1876 General Rascon issued rules for wood-cutting and ordered payment of one peso for each ton exported, but the impresarios laughed at the individuals commissioned to measure the wood. However, payment of the tax did increase to the amount of $3000. The current political chief, with your approval, reformed the rule and this year the impresarios have announced that a certain number of trees up to a limit will be counted against a set tax of $6, and with this method the taxes have gone up to $4200; but tax evasion goes on at a grand scale as I had the opportunity to find out on the visit I made to the ten mountain camps or logging camps that fortunately exist almost merged in an area of 10 leagues along the banks of the Lacantun River, a tributary of La Pasión. This could also convince me that with only the ten undertakings now established, logging should yield a product, through rents, of more than $8000, which could be added to each year as new undertakings are established.

I have made this constituent observation in each logging camp while accompanied by four others who proceeded into the heart of the forest to count the trees that had been cut and worked, while I examined the books on entries of running bills with the workmen and bookkeepers, which avoided the carrying out of Article 4 of the Workers' Law. With the information from the books and records and with the information that I derived, I was able to investigate everything and found that the first cutters to begin logging this year began on January 20; nevertheless, sir, by the 25th of May it appeared that not one of these establishments had cut less than 30 percent more than the number of trees for which they had paid, and the consequences of this breach of contract in November was that they cut 150 percent more timber than allowed and thereby defrauded the government of this amount. But the ease with which I verified these figures this year will not be possible in the coming year because they are always seeking means of avoiding detection, even mixing new stumps among the old so that they will not be counted, and they hide the books or do anything else possible to disorient those trying to collect bills.

As a consequence, it becomes necessary to make laws guaranteeing the national interest, giving these establishments security so that they may meet expenses, beginning with a guarantee of rights for several years and taking into account that the threat that the businesses will fail and that the houses of Tabasco will abandon trade by withdrawing credit are without reality; because neither will the impresarios retire because their businesses give them everything, nor will the merchant houses withdraw their credit when they have such great sums invested; and on the other hand, they would not want to abandon something that produces for them 35 or 40 percent of their capital, because they see that all they need to do is to pay four or six *reales* [previously used Central American currency. 1 peso = 8 reales] more for each ton of wood to reimburse the impresarios for the tax that they will no longer be cheating. If today the merchant houses of Tabasco pay the owners of logging camps 10 pesos per ton, or 12 if no debt is owed, then they will be paid 11 and 13 pesos and thus earn only 10 percent less, and above all, the wood loses no value; on the contrary, each day it brings better prices and only others who have paid a just value will sell.

I have the honor of presenting you with a map of the Usumacinta River, which I was given by Pedro D'Oliere, a resident of Sacluk, who was given the order by your *principales,* Jamet and Sastré of Tabasco. Sr. D'Oliere proposed that he continue to study the La Pasión River and the tributaries that form the Usumacinta.

The situation of the logging camps along the Lacantun River attracts one's attention because they have not been noticed previously, and are not marked on any of our worthless maps; such as those of Sonnerstein that give it the name Istatan. However, it is so torrential or at least more than the Chisoy (running parallel to it), and is known some 16 leagues from where it rises from its entrance into La Pasión. A certain Sr. Ballinas, employed at the house of Valenzuela of Tabasco, proposed to confirm or refute the idea that the Ococingo River in Chiapas empties into the Usumacinta, and he actually left Chiapas in his reconnaissance, going down the lower reaches of the river and determining that the Ococingo is a tributary of the Usumacinta. Consequently, this merchant house of Valenzuela proceeded to establish a logging camp on the Ococingo that would be connect-ed with another on the Lacantun, but they have not made known which of the tributaries of the Lacantun is the Ococingo, which will be revealed when the lumber that is being cut there floats downstream for export. One supposes that the Ococingo rises in the Department of Huehuetenango, a few leagues from the Lacantun and it would be easy to verify this, telling the political chief that commissioners will come from the villages along the frontier of the Petén to reconnoiter their rivers from the source to the confluence, and they can have no other outlet than the Lacantun, being that it is intermediate to the Chisoy River; and I do not doubt that this reconnaissance will produce great results for the Departments of Huehuetenango and the Petén through exploitation of the areas adjacent to that beautiful river, areas in which one encounters all native fruits, and especially cacao, in abundance, and approaching at the same time a department with sparse population that adjoins the other department.

Edwin Rockstroh, who is employed at the weather station in this city, has undertaken some very interesting studies concerning the Departments of the Petén, Huehuetenango, and Alta Verapaz, and he surveyed the places he visited. With data acquired from various people and that which he acquired in his travels, he has surveyed the boundaries of these three departments and gives an approximation of the course of the Lacantun River. I have the honor of forwarding to you a copy of this survey that Mr. Rockstroh has made available to me with the proposition of making evident the importance of doing a study and formal investigation of the Amelco, Santa Eulalia, and San Mateo Istatan Rivers, together with the Ococingo from the Lacantun, without knowing which of these is the main contributor. It would be very difficult to find such complete data for these studies as this gentleman has gathered.

Continuing downstream from the confluence of the Lacantun and the Usumacinta one encounters, at a distance of some 4 or 5 leagues, the first tribe of Lacandones. This tribe is composed of a few families, the rest of whom have dispersed throughout the highlands of the Petén, and others who have since united. They were established only a short time along the banks of the Lacantun, but they were established on the upper reaches of this river and then emigrated to La Pasión and the Usumacinta. Both sexes are seen in white clothing similar to that which our women wear while bathing. They have no houses and live beneath arbors that they call champas, which are abandoned each time a death occurs, others being built at another place. They do not flee from those who come to visit them, but, on the contrary, they borrow an extra abundance of food. They eat game and fish and have great fields of maize. They cultivate the plantain, some fruits and sugarcane, and they carry no other arms than the bow and arrow. A few leagues farther downstream, according to the information I have obtained, there are other tribes of *bravo* Indians that still maintain the custom of face painting, and who have only been visited by Don Pedro D'Oliere during the reconnaissance of the river we have discussed.

I have communicated the observations that I made in the logging camps to the political chief in order that he may order the suspension of operations for this year, inasmuch as the impresarios have taken that which they have bought, and if he believes it is appropriate, he may impose punishments on those who have violated the rules as well as the Workers' Law.

I believe that this information should be extended to commerce between the Petén and Belize. All of the money which in effect comes from Tabasco is expended for workers in the logging camps, and is then spent in Flores, generally for clothing, which in effect passes the money to Belize because the businessmen of the Petén stock nothing that can be sold in Belize, except for the occasional shipment of cattle.

The value of the goods that are brought to the Petén exceeds $20,000 annually, for an area that should produce 15,000 or 16,000 pesos, but those paid have never reached 3000.

Communications from Cobán should be expedited in order to open that marketing area to the people of the Petén, where they could buy items upon which taxes have already been paid and where they can realize some profit from their cattle and many other articles that they produce. Moreover, there is a great need to create a guard of four soldiers in charge of an official in Plancha de Piedra, and a similar force in San Juan, on the road from Xarché, to be on the alert for contraband.

It would not be difficult to open a road for horse travel from Flores to Cobán. This work has been given impetus through your orders, and with a bit more

eagerness on the part of the political chiefs of Cobán, through means allowed them by the President-General, from application of the money from leasing the salt mines of Nueve Cerros, can bring to a head in two years the section of road that passes through this department. With respect to the Petén, there is $700 for road building on deposit, a subscription I raised that with the labor of the contributors has given a beginning to the work of that chief, ordering him to make a preliminary review in order to see if means can be found to avoid the areas of mire. It does not matter that sometimes the people near Flores will be obligated to give major service to that which comes before the law. They will be the ones to benefit.

Enclosed for you, Sr. Minister, is a plan of the road from Cobán to Flores, and another from here to Cobán, so that you may learn the way via the Chisoy River, embarking on the Salinas River.

The road that leaves Sacluk for Tenocique in Tabasco has become very well traveled. With a small amount of money from the owners of logging camps and the people serving in Sacluk, the authorities in Tenocique have ordered it opened, or another road made that will speed means of communication.

I will conclude this report by informing the Minister of my visit to the ruins of Tical, by virtue of the order that you expressly communicated to me.

These ruins are situated to the north, about 12 leagues from the shores of the Lake. To make the journey we embarked with the political chief from Flores at five in the afternoon and arrived at the end of the lake at six the following morning. Here we found the animals that we had sent on ahead by land two days previously; and sure of finding the road because we had sent someone to cut it, we continued our march at 10:00, passing the night in the jungle where we found water. The following day we began our march at dawn; at 2 leagues we passed the margin of a ravine in which was discovered vestiges of ancient buildings that were probably a town; and we traveled no more than 2 more leagues and discovered, after a small eminence with a clearing, two huge towers that we admired for their height and which still belong to the ancient city. A few blocks away a ledge that lies across the road attracts one's attention, and looking at it one discovers that it extends on both sides and that it is made of stone and mortar. Then one begins to comprehend that the ancient wall of the city, which must have been eight or ten *varas* thick, has fallen down and the remains form the present boundary. Continuing along this same road one can see on the left vestiges of buildings; after recrossing the wall, which undoubtedly forms a circle, one arrives at the tiny village of Tical, which today is composed of seven families of Yucatecan Indians and three families of Lacandones. Prepared for the necessity of living several days among the ruins, we asked them about a path a family of Lacandones had made for a milpa. I entered the city accompanied by some natives of San José with the necessary tools.

After crossing the wall for the third time, one arrives at the first great building, located on the edge of a ravine. This consists of a square pyramid of stone and mortar, 22 *varas* high from the city side and 45 *varas* high from the base. Three of its sides are next to the edge of the ravine and they are much higher, and on the west side what is now destroyed forms a ramp where one can make the ascent by holding on to the roots of trees or by looking for stones for support. The summit of the pyramid is the base for a tower of two stories and 15 *varas* in height. The interior is a single room that is divided by three huge walls, each of three *varas* thickness, and great doors, one to the front of three *varas* height and two *varas* width, and two doorways in the interior. At the sides there are small rooms resembling cells about one *vara* wide, three *varas* deep, and four high. Still existing at one and two *varas* from the floor are holes about six inches square set with bars of ebony, which are perfectly preserved, which served as a latch.

Using ropes, and at the risk of falling, one can climb up the outside to the second story, this floor having only one room six *varas* long by three wide, since the walls are two and a half *varas* thick.

This structure was built of fine *talpuja* worked in the form of bricks—a very white material like plaster and extremely easy to carve.

At the foot of the ramp we encountered a round stone shaped like a millstone covering another rectangular stone three *varas* in length, one and one-third wide, and one *vara* thick. Supposing it to be the mouth of a well, we all together managed to turn it over, encountering directly beneath it the floor of the street made of the same material and perfectly paved with mortar. The huge stone served us thereafter as a writing and dining table. Having continued the excavation for two *varas* and convinced that there was nothing

to be found, we continued our reconnaissance of that street and a series of houses, some complete and some destroyed, all open and none shut, without anything inside worthy of attention. As we were making the path in the forest, we noticed that the street formed an irregular circle, and I understood that the city must have been surrounded by ravines. I ordered new paths made to the right, always arriving, at any rate, at a line of houses whose backs were against the ravine; discovering thereby that the walled entrance to the city, by the level part, was to the west, and that the tower which we had just visited was that which defended the wall to the north. I then proposed to investigate if there was a similar tower to the south. So we moved to that area across a series of buildings, more or less large, defending each other and the intermediate houses, until we arrived at another tower equal to the first, but higher. The beams of the doors of these towers, which form the lintels of the doors, were pulled out by a foreign doctor the year before last, and that which time and nature could not destroy with the great trees that had grown there this man has done, because the lack of beams has finished ruining these buildings. It is said that the engravings on these doors are the histories of the buildings, and they have been sent to Europe.

From the platform of this last tower we discovered in the distance another tower of great dimensions; and cutting a path to it we discovered what could be one of the tallest buildings in America. The pyramid is 150 *varas* at the base on the city side, and is 80 *varas* high. The tower is built upon the pyramid, 133 *varas* long at the base in front and 16 deep. It has five floors we calculated to be 25 *varas* high, because we could not get up to the roof. We barely got up to the third floor and breaking the ceiling, we ascended within it. In order to go up, there must have been an exterior stairway that could be reached by way of the openings in the walls (*ventanas*), because there was no interior communication between the floors. The walls are three and four *varas* thick; the interior rooms are always very small, formed by narrow triangular arches supported by small tie beams of *chico* wood, ebony, or *mora* in a perfect state of preservation.

As that doctor of whom I spoke had done, I pulled out the lintels of the principal door of this building, saving the carved part and removing with an axe the rest of the beam, to bring them to our museum with some small insignificant objects of stone and clay that we found; and I am certain that many other small objects might have existed in that abandoned city, and they have been removed by the Indians in the course of more than five centuries.

There are in that circular street curious objects that appear to be a type of altar, existing at intervals of 25 or 30 *varas*, and in front of each is a round stone like that of a mill sitting on one of its faces, and another, regular square stone with capricious figures, idols, and hieroglyphs two *varas* in height and one in width.

In all, one gathers that the city was a single fortification. Some of the houses are situated between the two towers, with openings behind, and the rest form squared rows in the center of which is a plaza, and its entrances are defended by small towers in such a manner that the place is a labyrinth of plazas defending each other. The city in general, which is more than a league across, is defended by great towers of which only three have been explored by Magistrate Modesto Méndez and Dr. Bernoulli, and today this great one by me.

After four days, and due to the illness of the political chief, we returned to Flores; and the route which we traveled in ten hours by land and twelve by water presents not a single difficulty for any traveler visiting those notable monuments so worthy of study by competent men.

It is very satisfying to travel and to learn; but painful to describe a trip if one is not competent. It is thus evident, Sr. Minister, that I am the first to confess that this tired informant cannot give an exact idea of the Department of the Petén, which was the purpose of the President and yourself in commissioning me with that as an objective, leaving me with the pleasure of having fulfilled my duty to the extent my intelligence permits me.

Reiterating to you, Sr. Minister, the protestations of my consideration and respect, I have the honor of signing myself

Your most sincere and loyal servant

Salvador Valenzuela

Inspector of Agriculture

References

Avendaño de Loyola, Andrés
1987   *Relation of Two Trips to Peten Made for the Conversion of the Heathen Ytaex and Cehaches*. Translated by Charles P. Bowditch and O. Guillermo Rivera, edited and with notes by Frank E. Comparato. Culver City, CA: Labyrinthos.

Berlin, Heinrich
1951   El templo de las inscripciones—VI—de Tikal. *Antropología e Historia de Guatemala* 3:33–54.

Broman, Vivian
1957   Field Notes. Tikal Project files. Philadelphia.

Cerezo Dardon, Hugo
1951   Breve historia de Tikal. *Antropología e Historia de Guatemala* 3:1–8.

Clark, John E.
1991a   Flintknapping and Debitage Disposal among the Lacandon Maya of Chiapas, Mexico. In *The Ethnoarchaeology of Refuse Disposal*, ed. Edward Staski and Livingstone D. Sutro, pp. 63–88. Anthropological Research Papers 42. Tempe: Arizona State University.

1991b   Modern Lacandon Maya Lithic Technology and Blade Workshops. In *Maya Stone Tools*, ed. Thomas R. Hester and Harry J. Shafer, pp. 251–65. Madison, WI: Prehistory Press.

Cook, Scott
1982   *Zapotec Stoneworkers: The Dynamics of Rural Simple Commodity Production in Modern Mexican Capitalism*. Washington, DC: University Press of America.

Cotter, John L.
1958   *Archaeological Excavations at Jamestown, Virginia*. Archaeological Research Series, Washington, DC: National Park Service, U.S. Department of the Interior.

Cowgill, George L.
1963   Postclassic Period Culture in the Vicinity of Flores, Petén, Guatemala. Ph.D. dissertation, Harvard University.

Graham, Ian
2002   *Alfred Maudslay and the Maya: A Biography*. Norman: University of Oklahoma Press.

Hammond, Norman
1987   The Discovery of Tikal. *Archaeology* 40(3): 30–37.

Hazard, James E.
1957   Field Notes. Tikal Project files. Philadelphia.

Jerabek, Carlos
1959   *Tikal: A Guide Book*. Guatemala: Guatemalan Tourist Guide.

Jones, Grant D.
1998   *The Conquest of the Last Maya Kingdom*. Stanford: Stanford University Press.

Lundell, C.L.
1937   *The Vegetation of Peten*. Carnegie Institute of Washington, Publication 476.

Maler, Teobert
1908   *Explorations in the Department of Petén, Guatemala, and Adjacent Regions: Topoxté, Yaxhá, Benque Viejo, Naranjo*. Memoirs of the Peabody Museum of Archaeology and Ethnology, Vol. 4, No. 2. Cambridge, MA.

1910   *Explorations in the Department of Petén, Guatemala, and Adjacent Regions: Motul de San José, Petén Itzá*. Memoirs of the Peabody Museum of Archaeology and Ethnology, Vol. 4, No. 3. Cambridge, MA.

1911   *Explorations in the Department of Petén, Guatemala, and Adjacent Regions: Tikal*. Memoirs of the Peabody Museum of Archaeology and Ethnology, Vol. 5, No. 1. Cambridge, MA.

Márquina, Ignacio
1951   *Arquitectura prehispánica*. Mexico: Instituto Nacional de Antropología e Historia.

Maudslay, A.P.
1889–1902   Archaeology, Vol. 3. In *Biologia Centrali-Americana*, ed. F.D. Godman and O. Salvin. London: R.H. Porter.

Maudslay, Anne Cary Morris, and A.P. Maudslay
1899   *A Glimpse of Guatemala and Some of the Ancient Monuments of Central America*. London: John Murray.

Méndez, Modesto
1955   Descubrimiento de las ruinas de Tikal. Informe del Corregidor del Petén Modesto Méndez, de 6 de marzo de 1848. *Antropología e Historia de Guatemala* 7:3–7.

Meyer-Holdampf, Valerie
1997   *Ein Basler unterwegs im Dschungel von Guatemala: Carl Gustav Bernoulli (1834–1878) Arzt, Botaniker und Entdecker der Tikal-Platten*. Basel: GS-Verlag.

Misdea, Sharon Aponte
2002   A Visual History of Archaeology at Tikal. *Expedition* 44(2): 36–44.

Moholy-Nagy, Hattula
1963   Field Notes. Tikal Project files. Philadelphia.

Morley, S.G.
1938   *The Inscriptions of Peten,* Vol. 1. Carnegie Institution of Washington, Publication 437.

Nelson, Margaret
1987 Contemporary Specializations and Marketing of Manos and Metates in the Maya Highlands. In *Lithic Studies Among the Contemporary Highland Maya,* ed. Brian Hayden, pp. 148–59. Tucson: University of Arizona Press.

Palka, Joel W.
2005   *Unconquered Lacandon: Ethnohistory and Archaeology of Indigenous Culture Change.* Gainesville: University Press of Florida.

Paul, Lois
1941   House and Household Centers of San Pedro La Laguna. Unpublished ms. in the possession of Edwin M. Shook, 1962.

Redfield, Robert, and Alfonso Villa Rojas
1934   *Chan Kom: A Maya Village.* Carnegie Institution of Washington, Publication 448.

Reed, Nelson
1964   The Caste War of Yucatan. Standford: Stanford University Press.

Reina, Rubén E.
1962   The Ritual of the Skull in Petén, Guatemala. *Expedition* 4(4):26–35.

1967   Milpas and Milperos: Implications for Prehistoric Times. *American Anthropologist* 69:1–20.

1977   Tikal Village, 19th Century. Unpublished manuscript in possession of the author.

Reina, Rubén E., and Robert M. Hill, II
1978   *The Traditional Pottery of Guatemala.* Austin: The University of Texas Press.

Schwartz, Norman B.
1990   *The Forest Society: A Social History of Peten, Guatemala.* Philadelphia: University of Pennsylvania Press.

Soza, José María
1970   *Monografía del Departamento de El Petén.* 2 vols. Guatemala: Editorial José de Pineda Ibarra.

Thompson, J.E.S.
1954   *The Rise and Fall of Maya Civilization.* Norman: University of Oklahoma Press.

1963   *Maya Archaeologist.* Norman: University of Oklahoma Press.

Thompson, Raymond H.
1958   *Modern Yucatecan Pottery Making.* Memoirs of the Society for American Archaeology 15. Salt Lake City, UT.

TIKAL REPORTS (see TR. 12: Appendix B)

TR. 1:   Shook, Edwin M.
1956   *Field Director's Report: The 1956 and 1957 Seasons.* Philadelphia: The University Museum, University of Pennsylvania.

TR. 5:   Shook, Edwin M., and William R. Coe
1961   *Numeration, Terminology, and Objectives.* Philadelphia: The University Museum, University of Pennsylvania.

TR. 10:   Reina, Rubén E.
1961   *The Abandonment of primacias by Itza of San Jose, Guatemala, and Socotz, British Honduras.* Philadelphia: The University Museum, University of Pennsylvania.

TR. 11:   Carr, Robert F., and James E. Hazard
1961   *Map of the Ruins of Tikal, El Petén, Guatemala.* Philadelphia: The University Museum, University of Pennsylvania.

TR. 12:   Coe, William R., and William A. Haviland
1982   *Introduction to the Archaeology of Tikal, Guatemala.* Philadelphia: The University Museum, University of Pennsylvania.

TR. 13:   Puleston, Dennis E., edited by William A. Haviland
1983   *The Settlement Survey of Tikal.* Philadelphia:: The University Museum, University of Pennsylvania.

TR. 19:   Haviland, William A., Marshall J. Becker, Ann Chowning, Keith A. Dixon, and Karl G. Heider
1985   *Excavations in Small Residential Groups of Tikal: Groups 4F-1 and 4F-2.* Philadelphia: The University Museum, University of Pennsylvania.

TR. 21:   Becker, Marshall J., Christopher Jones, and John McGinn
1999   *Excavations in Residential Areas of Tikal: Groups with Shrines.* Philadelphia: The University Museum, University of Pennsylvania.

TR. 25A: Culbert, T. Patrick
1993   *The Ceramics of Tikal: Vessels from the Burials, Caches, and Problematical Deposits.* Philadelphia: The University Museum, University of Pennsylvania.

TR. 27A: Moholy-Nagy, Hattula, with William R. Coe
2008   *The Artifacts of Tikal. Part A: Ornamental and Ceremonial Artifacts and Unworked Material.* Philadelphia: University of Pennsylvania Museum of Archaeology and Anthropology.

TR. 27B: Moholy-Nagy, Hattula
2003   *The Artifacts of Tikal. Part B: Utilitarian Artifacts and Unworked Material.* Philadelphia: University of Pennsylvania Museum of Archaeology and Anthropology.

TR. 33A: Jones, Christopher, and Linton Satterthwaite
1982   *The Monuments and Inscriptions of Tikal: The Carved Monuments.* Philadelphia: The University Museum, University of Pennsylvania.

Tozzer, A.M.
1911   *A Preliminary Study of the Prehistoric Ruins of Tikal, Guatemala.* Memoirs of the Peabody Museum of Archaeology and Ethnology, Vol. 5, No. 2. Cambridge, MA.

Valenzuela, Salvador
1951   Informe sobre el departemento del Petén, dirigido al Ministerio de Fomento el 1o. de junio de 1879. *Anales de la Sociedad de Geografía e Historia* 25:379–410. Guatemala.

Villa Rojas, Alfonso
1945   *The Maya of East Central Quintana Roo.* Carnegie Institution of Washington, Publication 559.

Wolfe, Walter M.
1901a   Toward Yucatán. *Juvenile Instructor* 36(12): 356–59.

1901b   Through the Jungle. *Juvenile Instructor* 36(13): 408–10.

1901c   On to Flores. *Juvenile Instructor* 36(17): 517–21.

1901d   To the Uttermost Camp. *Juvenile Instructor* 36(21): 661–64.

1901e   The Ruins of Tikal. *Juvenile Instructor* 36(22): 680–83.

1901f   Back to Civilization. *Juvenile Instructor* 36(23): 718–21.

1901g   Travel Diary of 1901, unpublished ms. in the L. Tom Perry Special Collections, Harold B. Lee Library at Brigham Young University. Provo, UT.

Wurman, Richard
1958   Field Notes. Tikal Project files. Philadelphia.

Summary in Spanish

El capítulo 1 presenta las investigaciones del Proyecto Tikal del Museo de la Universidad de Pennsylvania en la ciudad precolombiana entre 1956 y 1971. Durante la medición de las ruinas para el mapa del sitio, se descubrieron concentraciones de artefactos que pertenecieron a una aldea que existió en Tikal por un corto periodo durante el final de la década de 1870. Además, por medio del Proyecto se descubrieron materiales adicionales abandonados por algunos de los exploradores, arqueólogos y chicleros que visitaban Tikal durante los años después de su descubrimiento oficial en 1848.

El capítulo 2 presenta el patrón de asentamiento de la aldea de Tikal del siglo 19 y describe cada sitio en el cual fueron descubiertos artefactos de los siglos 19 y 20.

El capítulo 3 describe e ilustra todos los hallazgos recogidos en campo, inclusive los de piedra molida de moler, vidrio, metal, barro, vasijas de cerámica y palmas y árboles de fruta plantados por los aldeanos.

Trece appendices completan el informe. Algunos están incluidos en el libro, los demás están en el CD-ROM que lo acompaña. Estos appendices presentan la fuente de datos del informe, un resumen de las visitas a Tikal publicadas entre 1695 y 1956, cartas a la autora describiendo aspectos de hallazgos históricos, notas acerca de la cultura material de San José Petén, un informe de Walter Wolfe acerca de su visita a Tikal en 1901, investigaciones sobre dos botellas de vidrio encontradas en Tikal y una traducción en inglés del informe detallado del viaje de Salvador Valenzuela através del Petén en 1879 el cual incluyo una visita a la aldea de Tikal.

El informe contiene 29 ilustraciones en blanco y negro incluidas en el libro y 47 imágenes en color y blanco y negro en el CD-ROM.

Figures

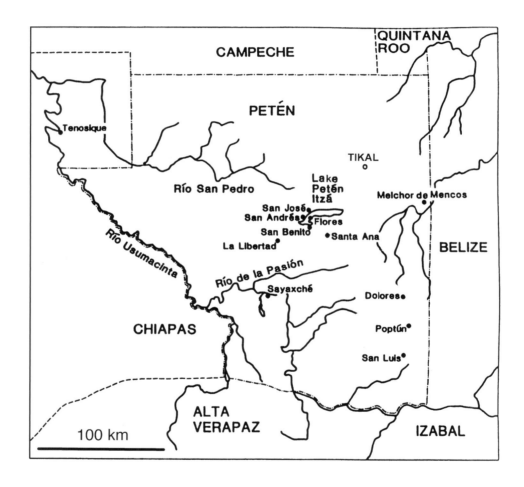

Figure 1. The Department of Petén, Guatemala. North is at the top of the map. After Schwartz 1990: Map 1. Reprinted with permission of the University of Pennsylvania Press.

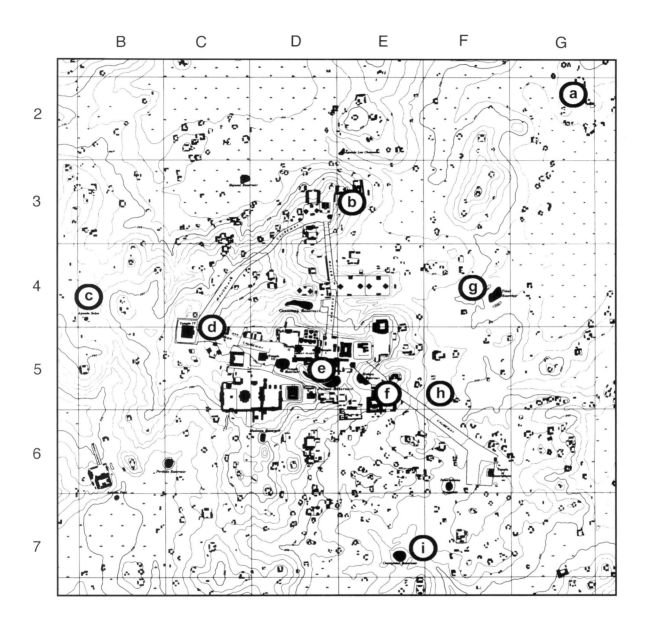

Figure 2. The central area of Tikal with the locations of Recent Sites and other Historic finds mentioned in the text.
a. RS 2G-1. *b.* Lot 1N/1. *c.* RS 4B-1. *d.* Lots 1C/8, 43C/2, and 43C/16. *e.* RS 5D-1 and 5D-2 on the Central Acropolis, Structure Group 5D-11. *f.* Structure Group 5E-11. *g.* RS 4F-1 through 4F-5 in the vicinity of the Tikal Aguada, the northern part of the 19th-century aldea at Tikal. *h.* RS 5F-1 through 5F-5, the southern part of the 19th-century aldea at Tikal. This part of the settlement was designated La Palmera by the Lacandon Archaeological Project (Palka 2005:154). *i.* RS 7E-1, near the Corriental Aguada. North is at the top of the map and each side of a Map Square measures 500 m.

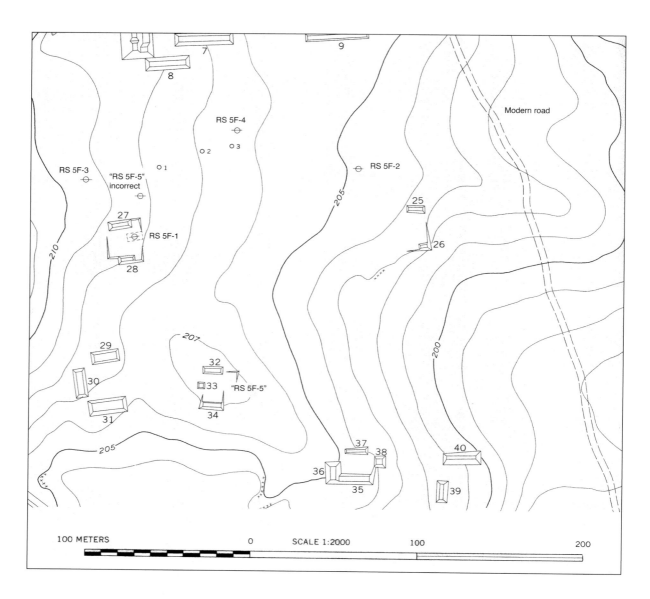

Figure 3. La Palmera, the southern portion of the 19th-century settlement at Tikal (see Fig. 2h).

Figure 4. The Tikal Aguada in 1956, before vegetation was removed and a new pier was constructed; cf. Figure L07. The Tikal Aguada was the principal water source for all post-Conquest visitors to Tikal, the 19th-century Tikal aldea, and the Tikal Project. Photograph by George Holten (Misdea 2002:39).

Figure 5. Great Temples IV (Str. 5C-4) and III (Str. 5D-3) photographed by A.P. Maudslay in 1881 or 1882 from the top of the roof comb of Great Temple I (Str. 5D-1); cf. Figure L04 (Maudslay and Maudslay 1899).

Figure 6. Great Temples III (Str. 5D-3), II (Str. 5D-2), and IV (Str. 5C-4) photographed from Great Temple I (Str. 5D-1) by A.P. Maudslay in 1881 or 1882 (Tozzer 1911: pl. 1); cf. Figure L05.

Figure 7. Great Temple III (Str. 5D-3) photographed by A.P. Maudslay in 1881 or 1882 (Tozzer 1911: pl. 4).

Figure 8. The campsite in the rain forest of the workers who accompanied the Maudslays to Tikal in 1881 or 1882. Note the pottery and gourd vessels on the ground, the storage of gear in hammocks, and bundles of other objects (food?) in nets affixed to tree trunks (Maudslay 1889–1902, Vol. 3: pl. 80b).

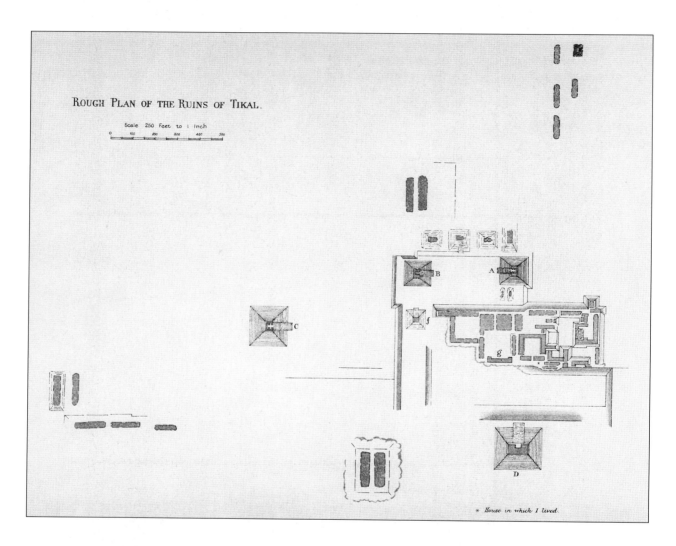

Figure 9. Sketch map of the center of Tikal by A.P. Maudslay. North is at the top. Str. 5D-52 where he set up camp, RS 5D-2, is the southern structure of the square assemblage of buildings in the approximate center of the Central Acropolis, Gp. 5D-11, marked with an x. Str. 5D-65, where Maler made his camp several years later, is the similarly oriented building to the west (Maudslay and Maudslay 1899).

Figure 10. RS 5D-2, looking east in Str. 5D-52, a Late Classic range structure on Tikal's Central Acropolis, Gp. 5D-11. The exterior of this gallery is shown on Figure L19. A wooden folding table and a box are visible among the furnishings (Maudslay 1889–1902, Vol. 3: pl. 80a).

Figure 11. RS 5D-2, looking east. The same gallery as seen in Figure 10. Teobert Maler took this photograph in 1895 or 1904. He described it as the fourth story of the Palace of the Five Stories, designated as Strs. 5D-50 and 5D-52 on the Tikal Map (TR. 11: Great Plaza Sheet). Maler placed a tripod metate and mano on the rear bench, a complete water jar near the central doorway, and two incomplete carved wooden tie beams against the rear wall (Tozzer 1911: pl. 10, 2).

Figure 12. RS 5D-2, looking west. Here Maler made a somewhat different arrangement of the artifacts shown in Figure 11 and added an incomplete water jar near the doorway. The tripod metate and mano on the bench were not recovered by the Tikal Project (Márquina 1951: Foto 247).

Figure 13. RS 5D-1. Teobert Maler shot this photograph of his temporary residence at Tikal in the gallery in Str. 5D-65, a Late Classic range structure in Group 5D-11, the Central Acropolis of Tikal. See Figures L21-L23 (Tozzer 1911: pl. 10, 1).

Figure 14. Pottery vessel forms from San José Petén, drawn from photographs taken by Margaret Arrott in the 1940s. Approximately 1:5 scale. *a,* Bowl with everted rim (*olla*); cf. Figure 28c-f. *b,* Bowl with solid lug handles (*tamalero*). The handles on this example appear to be incorrectly drawn; cf. Figures 28a,b, L26. *c,* Baking dish set cover (*tapadera*); cf. Figure 26b. *d,* Jar with strap handles (*cántaro*); cf. Figure 26c. *e,* Pitcher (*batidor*); cf. Figure 26d, e. *f,* Jar (*cántaro*) with loop handles; cf. Figure 27a-d (Reina and Hill 1978: fig. 41).

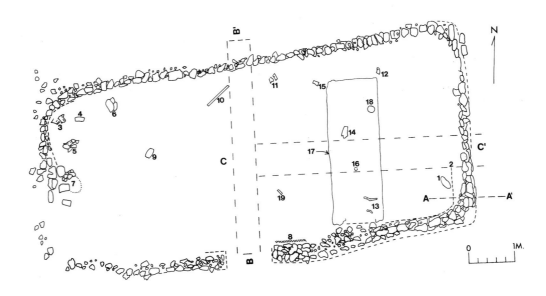

Figure 15. Plan of RS 5F-1, lots 1D/6 and 34A/1-14, a residence and possible church. A number of items were recovered from the floor of this house, the only RS house recorded by the Tikal Project with stone wall footings that permitted the identification of its plan; cf. Figures L33-L35. (1) charcoal deposit, (2) estimated line of the inner wall face, (3) fragments of a pottery bowl (Fig. 28c), (4) metate fragment (Fig. 21b), (5) mano (Fig. 18f) and sherds, (6) group of nested sherds, (7) hearth with burned stones, (8) two pieces of charcoal along the wall base, (9) mano (Fig. 18e), (10) shotgun barrel (Fig. 23a), (11) two machete fragments (Fig. 24, bottom, and 25c, top), (12) pottery pestle (Fig. 25f), (13) box strap fragments (Fig. 24), (14) metate fragment (not illustrated), (15) machete fragment (Fig. 25c, bottom), (16) charcoal, (17) Feature A, a rectangular patch of plaster, (18) a hole 8 cm in diameter in Feature A, (19) box strap fragment. Sections A-C are shown in Figure 16. Drawing by Barbara Hayden from a field drawing by Christopher Jones and William R. Coe.

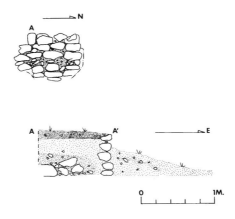

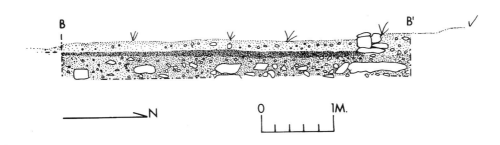

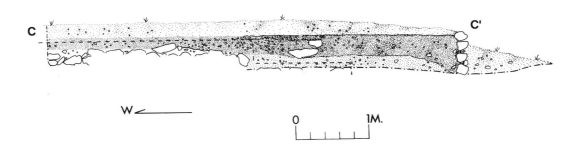

Figure 16. RS 5F-1, lots 1D/6 and 34A/1-14. Sections through the floor and foundations of the house shown on Figure 15. The 19th-century house was built upon the platform of a Classic Period residence, Str. 5F-27. Drawing by Barbara Hayden from a field drawing by William R. Coe.

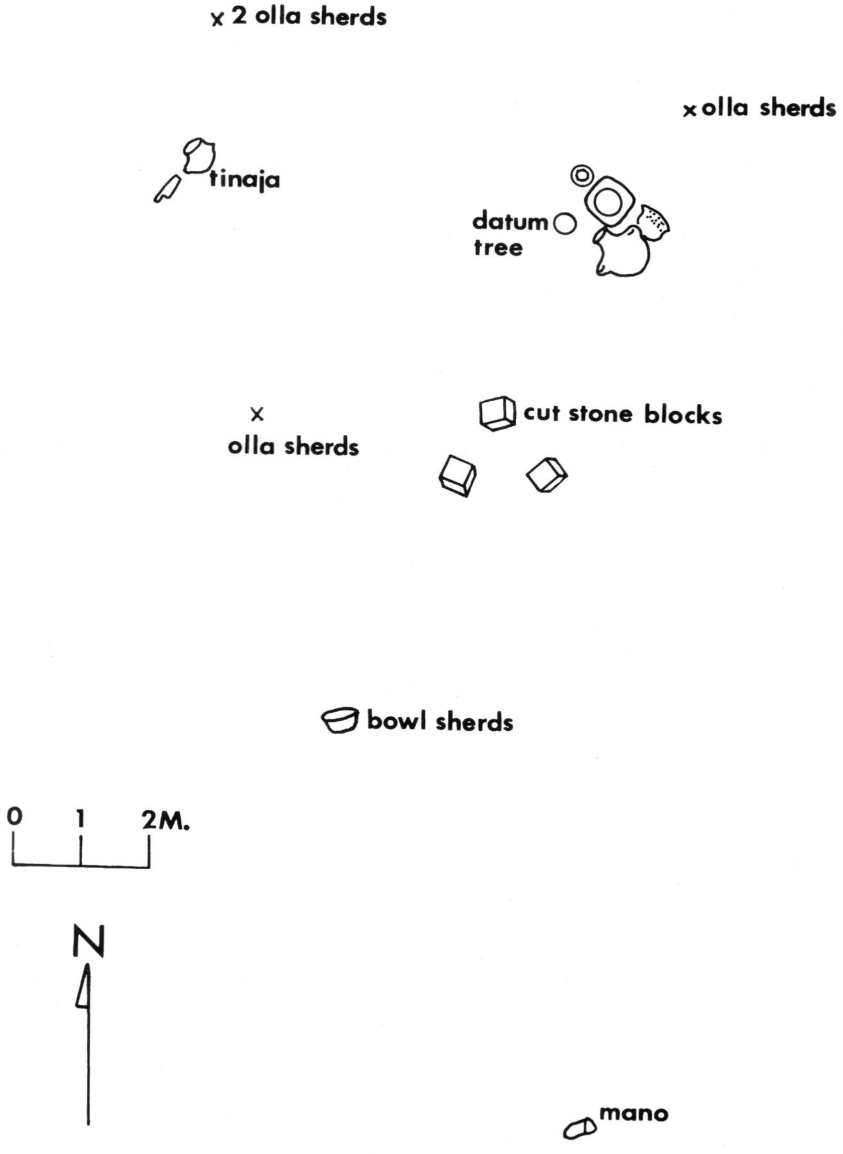

x **2 olla sherds**

x **olla sherds**

tinaja

datum tree ◯

x
olla sherds

▢ **cut stone blocks**

▱ **bowl sherds**

0   1   2M.

N

mano

Figure 17. RS 5F-2, lot 1D/3, a residence built of completely perished material. The plan shows the location of reconstructable pottery vessels (Figs. 27f, 28a), a cluster of two dolomite mortars (the best preserved is illustrated in TR. 27B: fig. 91c), a complete water jar (Fig. 27a), and a hearth of three cut-stone blocks; cf. Figure L36. Drawing by Barbara Hayden from a field drawing by Vivian Broman.

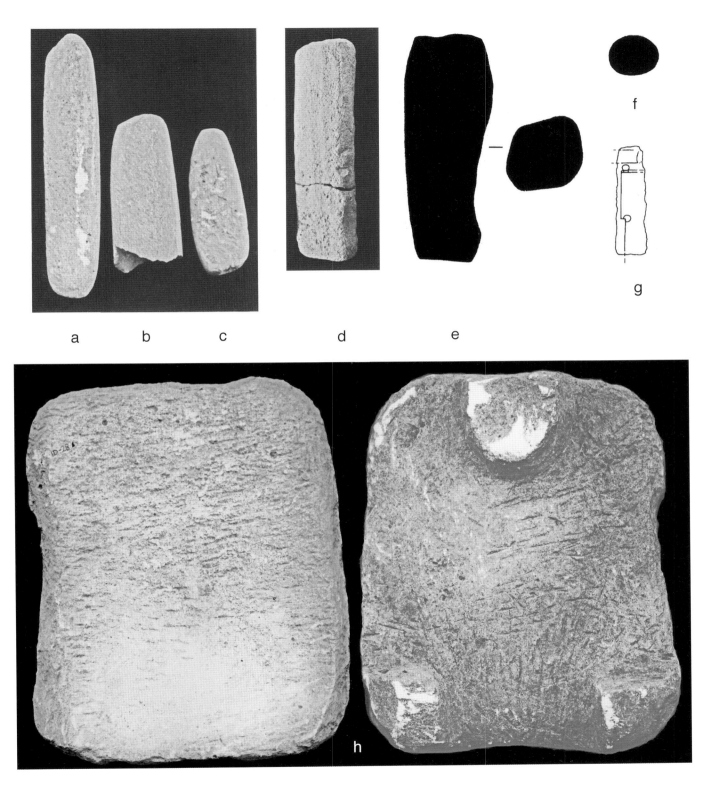

Figure 18. Manos and metates (1:4 scale except for 18g). *a-g,* Manos: *a,* 1C-37/9. *b,* 1D-7/3. *c,* 1C-46/9. *d,* 2B-20/3. *e,* Long and cross sections, 34A-4/2. *f,* Cross section, 34A-3/2. *g,* Shaped from a fragment of Stela 6 (TR. 33A: fig. 10c), 12B-275/283/1. Greatest length ca. 36 cm. *h,* Tripod metate, with metal tool marks on the grinding face and base, 1D-28/1.

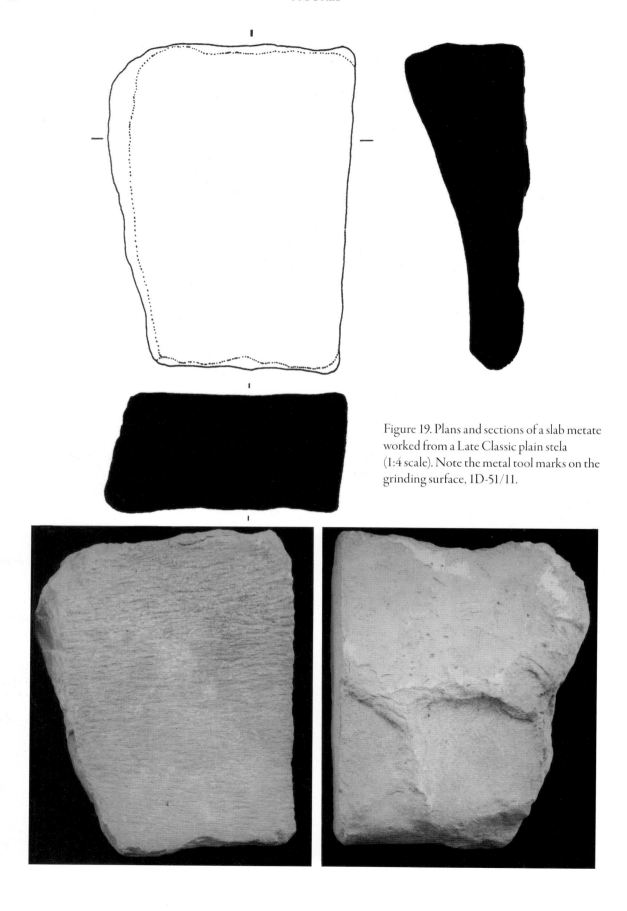

Figure 19. Plans and sections of a slab metate worked from a Late Classic plain stela (1:4 scale). Note the metal tool marks on the grinding surface, 1D-51/11.

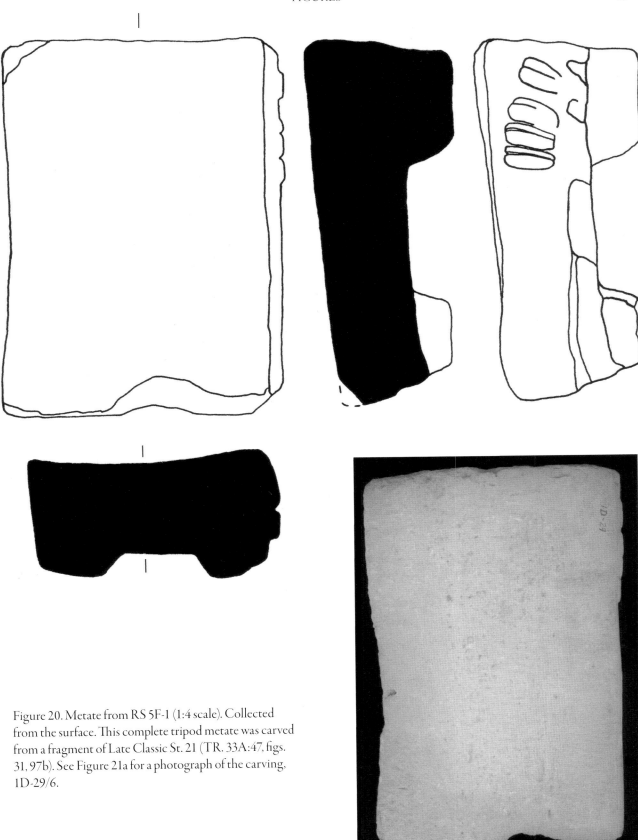

Figure 20. Metate from RS 5F-1 (1:4 scale). Collected from the surface. This complete tripod metate was carved from a fragment of Late Classic St. 21 (TR. 33A:47, figs. 31, 97b). See Figure 21a for a photograph of the carving, 1D-29/6.

Figure 21. Metates and other ground stone artifacts (1:4 scale except 21c at 1:10 scale). *a,* Metate made from St. 21, 1D-29/6. *b,* Metate fragment, 34A-9/2. *c,* Uncatalogued metate from Early Classic altar fragment, TR. 33A:65k. *d,* Unclassified limestone artifact, 1A-1/1. *e,* Slab metate from a monument fragment, 1D-4/1. *f,* Battered limestone ball, 1D-27/3.

a   b   c   d   e   f   g

n   i   j   k   l

Figure 22. Glass bottles, an iron
cooking pot, and hand mill (1:4 scale).
a-k, Glass bottles: *a,* 1C-51/1.
b, 1D-8a/4. *c,* 1D-55a/11. *d,* 1D-55b/11.
e, 1D-58/9. *f,* 1C-32/8. *g,* Uncatalogued, unprovenienced beer bottle.
h, 1D-8b/4. *i,* 1D-39/10. *j,* 43C-65/32.
k, 43C-66/16. *l,* Iron cooking pot,
1D-70/9A. *m,* Iron hand mill for grinding corn, 1D-78a, b/12.

m

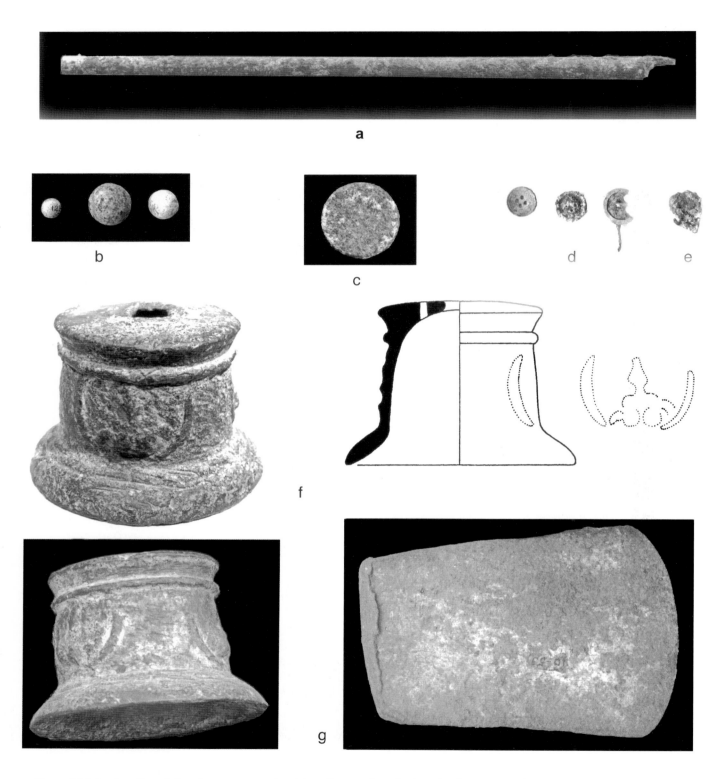

Figure 23. Metal artifacts (1:2 scale except *a* at 1:4 scale). *a,* Shotgun barrel, 34A-5/2. *b,* Three gun shot, 12B-49/9, 2B-6/1, and 2B-7/1. *c,* Metal pillbox, 1D-54/11. *d,* Three metal buttons, 34A-17/2, 34A-22/6, 34A-20/1. *e,* Flat metal fragment, 34A-6b/2. *f,* Three views of a small bronze bell, 1D-12/4. *g,* Axe head, 1D-53/11.

Figure 24. Metal box strap and machete fragments (1:2 scale). Eight thin metal box strap fragments, including a fragment with two nails, 34A-8/2 and 34A-11/2, cf. Figure L35. A machete fragment is to the immediate right of the strap fragment with two nails, 34A-10/2, and another machete fragment is in the bottom row, left, 34A-6a/2; see also Figure 25c.

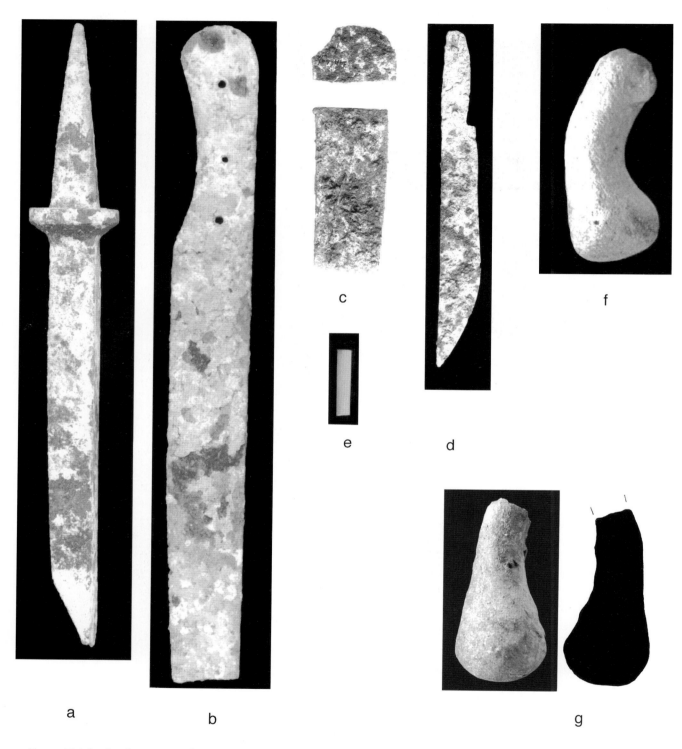

Figure 25. Metal and pottery artifacts (1:2 scale). *a,* Chisel, 44A-34/11. *b,* Collins type of machete fragment, 1D-18/3. *c,* Lagarto type of machete fragment at top, 34A-6a/2, and Collins type of machete fragment at bottom, 34A-10/2; see also Figure 24. *d,* Large knife, 117C-6/3. *e,* Pottery pipe stem fragment, white paste, 4J-2/1. *f,* Whole pottery pestle with a nose-like projection on the handle, 34A-7/2. *g,* Two views of a pestle end fragment, 1D-11/7.

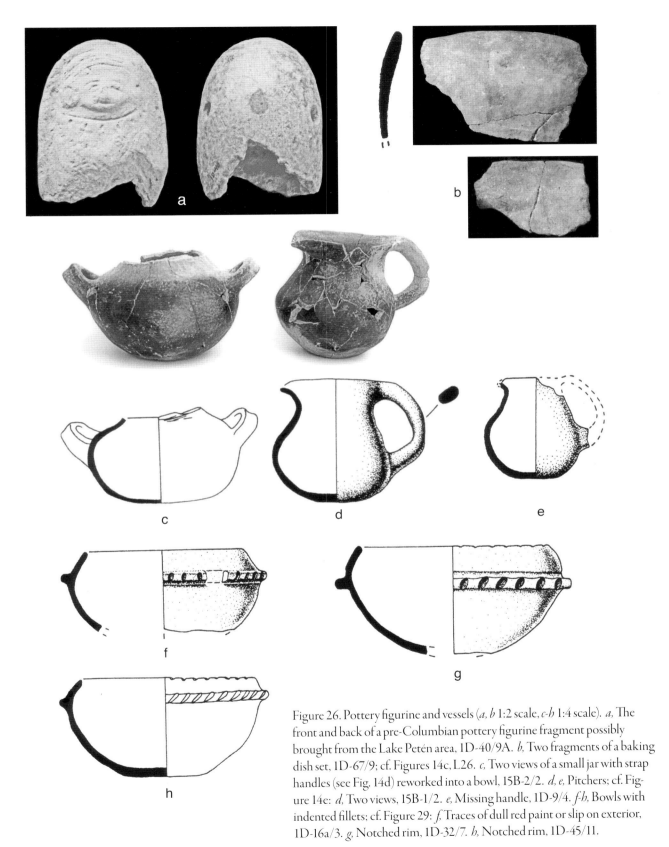

Figure 26. Pottery figurine and vessels (*a, b* 1:2 scale, *c-h* 1:4 scale). *a,* The front and back of a pre-Columbian pottery figurine fragment possibly brought from the Lake Petén area, 1D-40/9A. *b,* Two fragments of a baking dish set, 1D-67/9; cf. Figures 14c, L26. *c,* Two views of a small jar with strap handles (see Fig. 14d) reworked into a bowl, 15B-2/2. *d, e,* Pitchers; cf. Figure 14e: *d,* Two views, 15B-1/2. *e,* Missing handle, 1D-9/4. *f-h,* Bowls with indented fillets; cf. Figure 29: *f,* Traces of dull red paint or slip on exterior, 1D-16a/3. *g,* Notched rim, 1D-32/7. *h,* Notched rim, 1D-45/11.

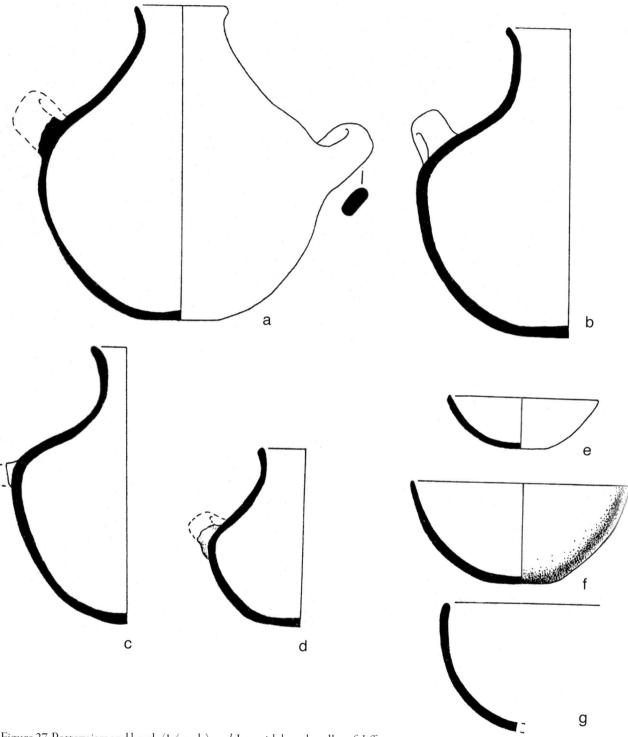

Figure 27. Pottery jars and bowls (1:4 scale). *a-d,* Jars with loop handles of different sizes; cf. Figure 14f: *a,* 1D-22/3. *b,* 1D-13/2. *c,* 34A-1/2. *d,* 1D-64/9. *e-g,* Bowls, cf. Figures L27, L28: *e,* Small flaring-sided bowl, 1D-46/11. *f,* Flaring-sided bowl, 1D-14/3. *g,* Fragment of a round-sided bowl, diameter uncertain, 1D-60/9.

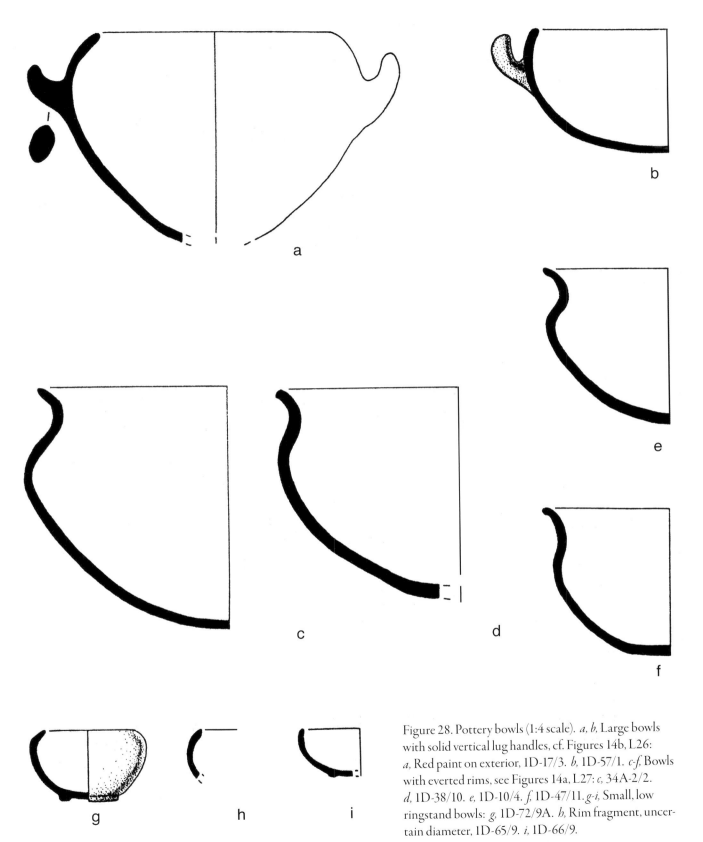

Figure 28. Pottery bowls (1:4 scale). *a, b,* Large bowls with solid vertical lug handles, cf. Figures 14b, L26: *a,* Red paint on exterior, 1D-17/3. *b,* 1D-57/1. *c-f,* Bowls with everted rims, see Figures 14a, L27: *c,* 34A-2/2. *d,* 1D-38/10. *e,* 1D-10/4. *f,* 1D-47/11. *g-i,* Small, low ringstand bowls: *g,* 1D-72/9A. *h,* Rim fragment, uncertain diameter, 1D-65/9. *i,* 1D-66/9.

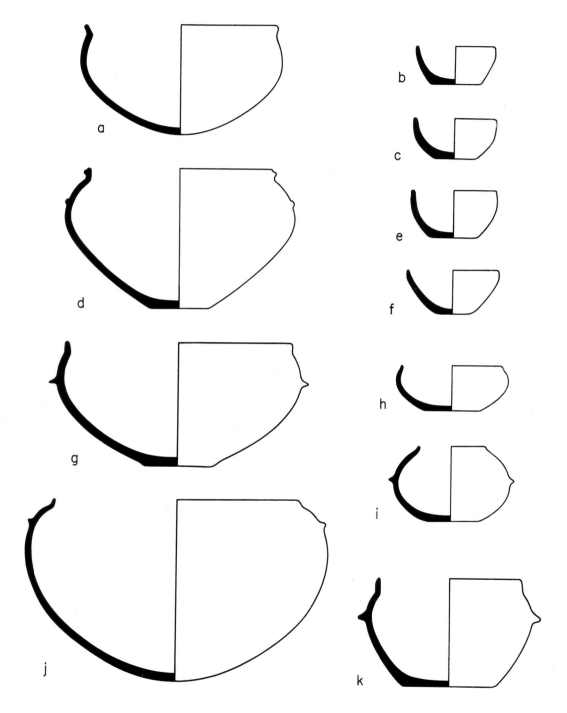

Figure 29. Pottery bowls from Yucatán (1:5 scale). A sample of large and small bowls produced in various parts of the peninsula in the 1950s. Note the fillet decoration on *d, g,* and *j* (Thompson 1958: fig. 12). Reproduced by permission of the Society for American Archaeology.

Tables

TABLE 2.1. Summary of Tikal Recent Sites

Recent Site	Lot number	Description	Probable occupation
RS 2G-1	1D/11	house	Tikal aldea
RS 4B-1	1D/10	camp	chicleros
RS 4F-1	1D/2	water jars	Tikal aldea
RS 4F-2	1D/9	house or houses	Tikal aldea
RS 4F-3	1D/1	house or houses	Tikal aldea
RS 4F-4	1A/1, 1D/4	probable house, part of RS 4F-3	Tikal aldea
RS 4F-5	1D/9A	part of RS 4F-2 and/or a probable house	Tikal aldea
RS 5D-1	15B/2	temporary residence	Teobert Maler
RS 5D-2	44A/3, 44A/11	temporary residence	A.P. Maudslay
RS 5F-1	1D/6, 34A/1-14	residence/church	Tikal aldea
RS 5F-2	1D/3	two houses	Tikal aldea
RS 5F-3	1D/7	one or two houses	Tikal aldea
RS 5F-4	1D/8	probable house	Tikal aldea
RS 7E-1	1D/12	probable house	Tikal aldea

TABLE 2.2. Distribution of Traits (Tikal Project Only)
* Not Collected, x Present

Recent Site	Multi-stone hearths	Citrus trees	Other exotic trees	Manos	Slab or tripod metates	Other Recent stone artifacts	pre-Columbian stone tools	Other pre-Columbian artifacts	Glass bottles	"China"	Machetes	Shotgun part	Shot	Buttons	Box strap fragments	Metal cooking pots	Other metal artifacts	Axe head	Chisel	Pottery pestles	Pipe	Baking dish (comal/tapadera)	Small plain bowls	Small ringstand bowls	Pitchers	Water jars	Indented-fillet bowls	Large bowls, no handles	Large bowls, lug handles	Unworked bone fragments	Wooden artifact fragment
RS 2G-1					1		1		2								1	1					1			1	1	3			
RS 4F-1		x																								2					
RS 4F-2		x			2		x		1													1	1	1		1		4			
RS 4F-3		x					x	1																		x		3	1		
RS 4F-4		x				1		x	2							1									1			1			
RS 4F-5		x	x				x																	1	1						
RS 5F-1	1	x	x	2	2	1	x	x		1	2	1		3	x		2			1						1		2	1	2	1
RS 5F-2	2	x	x	1		1	x				1												1			2	1	4	1		
RS 5F-3	2	x	x				x													1						1	1	2			
RS 5F-4*	1				1																										
RS 7E-1*		x			1						1						1														
RS 5D-1																			1						1	1					
RS 5D-2									1																	1					
RS 4B-1	x																											1			
Recent		x	x	4	1				4				3			1	3				1										

TABLE 2.3. Concordance of Recent Sites Defined by the University of Pennsylvania Museum's Tikal Project and the Lacandon Archaeological Project Operations at La Palmera (Palka 2005: Map 6.4; TR. 11: Camp Quadrangle)

La Palmera	Recent Site
1	-
2	5F-3
3	5F-3
4	-
5	5F-2
6	5F-2
7	5F-1
8	-

Index

Page numbers in italics indicate figures; L-numbers are figures on the CD.